FROM MONOBANK TO
COMMERCIAL BANKING

The **Nordic Institute of Asian Studies** (NIAS) is a research and service institute located in Copenhagen where it collaborates closely with Copenhagen University and the Copenhagen Business School as well as with Lund University in Sweden and the wider Nordic Asian Studies community. Funded in part by the governments of Denmark, Finland, Iceland, Norway and Sweden via the Nordic Council of Ministers and in part directly by the Nordic scholarly community, NIAS works to encourage and support Asian Studies in the Nordic countries as well as actively participating in the international scholarly community in its own right. In so doing, NIAS has published books since 1969 and in 2002 launched **NIAS Press** as an independent, not-for-profit publisher aiming at a premium reputation among authors and readers for relevant and focused, quality publishing in the field of Asian Studies.

The **Institute of Southeast Asian Studies** (ISEAS) was established as an autonomous organization in 1968. It is a regional centre dedicated to the study of socio-political, security and economic trends and developments in Southeast Asia and its wider geostrategic and economic environment.

The Institute's research programmes are Regional Economic Studies (RES, including ASEAN and APEC), Regional Strategic and Political Studies (RSPS), and Regional Social and Cultural Studies (RSCS).

ISEAS Publications, an established academic press, has issued more than 1,000 books and journals. It is the largest scholarly publisher of research about Southeast Asia from within the region. ISEAS Publications works with many other academic and trade publishers and distributors to disseminate important research and analyses from and about Southeast Asia to the rest of the world.

FROM MONOBANK TO COMMERCIAL BANKING

Financial Sector Reforms in Vietnam

Jens Kovsted, John Rand and Finn Tarp

With Nguyen Dinh Tai, Nguyen Van Huong,
Ta Minh Thao and Luu Duc Khai

NIAS
Press

INSTITUTE OF SOUTHEAST ASIAN STUDIES
Singapore

First published in 2005 by NIAS Press
Nordic Institute of Asian Studies
Leifsgade 33, DK–2300 Copenhagen S, Denmark
tel: (+45) 3532 9501 • fax: (+45) 3532 9549
E-mail: books@nias.ku.dk • Website: www.niaspress.dk

First published in 2005 in Singapore by
Institute of Southeast Asian Studies (ISEAS)
30 Heng Mui Keng Terrace, Pasir Panjang, Singapore 119614
E-mail: publish@iseas.edu.sg • Website: http://bookshop.iseas.edu.sg
for distribution in the ASEAN countries, Japan, Korea, Taiwan,
Australia and New Zealand.

Original publication of this work was assisted by financial support
from the Danish Ministry of Foreign Affairs (Danida)

British Library Cataloguing in Publication Data
From monobank to commercial banking : financial sector
  reforms in Vietnam. - (NIAS reports ; no. 48)
  1.Ngan hang nha nuoc Viet Nam 2.Banks and banking -
  Vietnam 3.Vietnam - Economic conditions - 1975-
  5.Vietnam - Economic policy - 1975-
  I.Kovsted, Jens II.Rand, John III.Tarp, Finn, 1951-
  332.1'09597'09049

ISBN 87-91114-62-4 (NIAS hbk edition)
ISBN 87-91114-86-1 (NIAS pbk edition)
ISBN 981-230-290-5 (ISEAS edition)

Typesetting by Translations ved LJ
Printed and bound in Singapore

Contents

Abbreviations ... viii

Preface ... xi

Introduction ... xvii

CHAPTER 1
Central planning and the first phase of reforms ... 1

CHAPTER 2
The East Asian Financial Crisis and its aftermath, 1997–2003 ... 33

CHAPTER 3
A regional comparison of bank supervision and regulation ... 57

CHAPTER 4
The State Bank of Vietnam ... 79

CHAPTER 5
Financial services for the agricultural sector ... 121

Chapter 6
Conclusion ... 135

Appendices
A. The state-owned commercial banks ... 139
B. Important events, 1988–2003 ... 142
C. Bank supervision and regulation indicators ... 147

References ... 155

Index ... 161

LIST OF TABLES

1.1: Legal origin, political system and initial endowments ... 6

1.2: Commercial banks ... 13

1.3: Foreign currency credit to state and non-state enterprises ... 19

1.4: Lending to non-state institutions ... 20

1.5: Sources of credit in survey of 707 SMEs ... 30

2.1: Market share of life insurance companies ... 40

2.2: Overall credit growth and credit growth to the SOEs ... 42

2.3: Non-performing loans ... 43

2.4: SOE equitisation targets and transformations to date ... 45

2.5: Recapitalisation of SOCBs ... 47

2.6: Ratio of non-performing loans to total loans ... 49

2.7: Dong depreciation to the dollar, 1992–2001 ... 51

2.8: USBTA Commitments in the banking sector ... 52

3.1: Financial sector concentration in East Asia ... 61

3.2: Financial sector concentration in a global perspective ... 62

3.3: Bank entry regulation in East Asia ... 65

3.4: Bank entry regulation in a global perspective ... 66

3.5: Official supervisory variables in East Asia ... 68

3.6: Official supervisory variables in a global perspective ... 70

3.7: Legal restrictions on banking activity in East Asia ... 71

3.8: Legal restrictions on banking activity in a global perspective ... 71

3.9: Capital regulatory variables in East Asia ... 73

3.10: Capital regulatory variables in a global perspective ... 74

4.1: Turnover rate of central bank governors ... 86

4.2: The market for treasury bills ... 92

4.3: SBV supervision before and after the Law on the State Bank – I ... 99

4.4: SBV supervision before and after the law on the State Bank – II ... 100

4.5: NPLs in East Asia in 1998 ... 107

4.6: AMC set-up in East Asian countries ... 108

4.7: Operational funding for AMCs in East Asia ... 115

5.1: Key characteristics of financial institutions in the agricultural sector ... 125

LIST OF FIGURES

1.1: Inflation ... 11

1.2: Credit to SOEs and private enterprises ... 19

1.3: Annual GDP growth ... 22

1.4: Gross domestic savings ... 23

1.5: Foreign currency deposits ... 25

2.1: Foreign direct investments, net inflows ... 34

4.1: The structure of the Vietnamese AMC system ... 111

5.1: VBARD allocation of credit in 2000 ... 123

Abbreviations

ADB	Asian Development Bank
AMC	asset management company
ASEAN	Association of South East Asian Nations
BSP	Bank for Social Policies
CAMEL	capital, asset, management, earnings and liquidity of banks
CAR	capital adequacy ratio
CC	credit cooperative
CCF	Central Credit Fund
CIC	Credit Information Centre
CIEM	Central Institute for Economic Management
DAF	Development Assistance Fund
DIA	Deposit Insurance Agency
EAFC	East Asian Financial Crisis, 1997–98
FDI	foreign direct investment
FLC	Financial Lease Company
FRA	Financial Sector Restructuring Authority
GDP	gross domestic product
GDS	gross domestic savings
GNP	gross national product
IAS	international accounting standards

ICB	Incombank
ICVB	Industrial and Commercial Bank of Vietnam
IDCM	inter-bank domestic currency market
IFAD	International Fund for Agricultural Development
IMF	International Monetary Fund
JSB	joint stock bank
LDC	less-developed country
LEIPC	legislative and executive index of political competitiveness
LCF	Local Credit Fund
LUR	land use rights
MOF	Ministry of Finance
MOJ	Ministry of Justice
MPI	Ministry of Planning and Investment
NIAS	Nordic Institute of Asian Studies
NPL	non-performing loan
PCF	People's Credit Fund
PCPI	prompt corrective power index
PM	Prime Minister's Office
RAB	Radhanasin Bank
RCF	Regional Credit Fund
RCST	Registry Centre for Secured Transactions
Rosca	Rotating Savings and Credit Association
SBV	State Bank of Vietnam
SME	small and medium-scale enterprise
SOB	state-owned bank
SOCB	state-owned commercial bank

SOE	state-owned enterprise
SSC	State Security Commission
T-Bills	treasury bills
TOR	turnover rate (of Central Bank governors)
US	United States
USBTA	US–Vietnam Bilateral Trade Agreement
VAS	Vietnamese accounting standards
VAT	value added tax
VBARD	Vietnam Bank of Agriculture and Rural Development
VBID	Vietnamese Bank for Investment and Development
VBP	Vietnam Bank of the Poor
VCB	Vietcombank
VCP	Vietnamese Communist Party
VLSS	Vietnamese Living Standards Survey
VPSC	Vietnam Postal Service Savings Company
WBG	World Bank Group
WDI	world development indicators
WTO	World Trade Organisation

Preface

In terms of level of economic development, Vietnam has made significant progress over the past decade. Standards of living have improved significantly, and the country's socio-economic achievements are impressive from a human development perspective. One of the main drivers of economic growth and development has been the implementation of various economic reforms, initiating the transformation from a centrally coordinated and planned economy towards a more market-orientated system. Although the uncertainty and lower economic growth following in the wake of the Asian Financial Crisis caused a temporary slowdown of the reform process, the momentum appears to have picked up again in recent years.

The financial sector takes centre stage in the renewed efforts to reform the Vietnamese economy, in part because of the extensive linkages between the predominantly state-owned banking sector and the crisis-stricken state-owned enterprises (SOEs); and in part because the creation of a more market-based financial sector is expected to improve the mobilisation of savings, the diversification of risks, and the allocation of resources in the economy. The current and planned reforms of the financial sector, however, also represent an opportunity to initiate a deeper and more structural break in the way in which the Vietnamese economy is managed.

Only 15 years ago, during the era of central coordination and planning, the financial sector was completely subordinate and instrumental to the achievement of government objectives in the productive, state-owned sectors. Although the Vietnamese government has stopped using the financial sector as a direct instrument for the implementation of productive sector policies, considerable indirect government control of financial sector activities persists. It is in this context that the recently initiated round of reforms potentially holds the promise of lessening the persistent (indirect) government control through the creation of a more market-based, autonomous financial sector.

As indicated by its title, this study will focus on banks: primarily on the state-owned banks. This is not equivalent to saying that other parts of the sector are not important. They are, but regardless of developments in the near future, banks will continue to be the dominant source of outside funding in Vietnam – thus justifying focusing primarily on one type of financial institution.

A first version of this study is available as CIEM discussion paper (CIEM Discussion Paper 0301) published in January 2003. Work on this first version was completed during the autumn of 2002; the last comprehensive study of the financial sector in Vietnam had been made seven earlier (World Bank 1995). As a consequence, the objective of the first version of the study was to remedy the shortage of comprehensive financial sector analyses in Vietnam. It is, however, important to point out that the first version of the study was by no means intended to be a follow-up to the 1995 World Bank report or to substitute for the World Bank Banking Sector Review published towards the end of 2002. While the publication of the latter (World Bank 2002) naturally provided an occasion to review the first version of this study, it by no means rendered it superfluous. One example is the issue of non-performing loans (NPL). Following an initial acknowledgement that the level of NPLs accumulated in the banking system is of concern, the World Bank (2002a) goes on to note that since 'the restructuring and the recapitalization program undergoes frequent joint reviews by the SBV, the IMF and the World Bank Group (WBG), this exercise (i.e. the World Bank Report) will refrain from commenting directly on the plans and the progress, but it will instead take stock independently of the status of the banking reform process.' However, as the above mentioned 'frequent joint reviews' are not made available to the public, the fact that the most recent World Bank report abstains from analysing the NPL problem creates a vacuum. As a consequence, Chapter 6 in this study looks into the central issues surrounding the ongoing process to resolve the NPL problem.

The present study is thus an updated and substantially revised version of the earlier CIEM discussion paper. The objectives are twofold: first, to help establish an open dialogue about the nature and speed of the financial sector reforms in Vietnam based on recurrent independent assessments of banking sector issues and problems; second (and not unrelated to the first objective), to focus on some the issues not dealt with by previous studies of the financial sector in Vietnam.

The above mentioned unavailable 'joint reviews' directs attention to the lack of transparency surrounding issues related to the financial sector in Vietnam. This lack includes both key measures of financial sector performance (such as, for example the ratio of NPL to total loans as measured by international accounting standards) and the government decision-making processes and strategies of relevance to the financial sector (e.g. the extent of continued policy lending through state-owned commercial banks). In both areas outsiders are presented with an information policy that comes close to opaque closure. This is most likely in part attributable to the Vietnamese culture of consensus governance (see Chapter 3). Another possible explanation for the lack of transparency rests on a conjecture that the financial sector (through the above mentioned NPLs and the continued close relationship between state-owned banks and state-owned companies) holds an 'uncollected bill' for failed past policies. To the extent that this conjecture is correct, the high priority assigned to social and political stability by the government in turn implies that the government has little incentive to reveal the true size of this problem. Regardless of the explanations given, the lack of transparency represents a real problem which we seek to overcome by using as many independent sources of information as possible. Any remaining uncertainty will be noted throughout the study as will failure to obtain relevant information.

The noted factual and empirical ambiguity does, however, not disappear when we instead turn to look for an established, commonly agreed upon framework for financial sector analyses.

Establishing a common ground among economists analysing this sector and its role in generating economic growth and stability is at best difficult. Views range from support to Joan Robinson's claim that 'where enterprise leads finance follows' (Robinson 1980), to those like King and Levine (1993) who hold that Schumpeter was right to suggest that financial intermediaries promote and accelerate economic growth through the identification of and subsequent allocation of funds to high-growth investments. This lack of analytical coherence also extends to more specific policy-related decisions such as: (i) whether transitional economies should develop a securities market-based financial system (such as that in place in the United States) or instead opt for a bank-based system (found in Germany), and (ii) whether central bank autonomy should be strengthened through the legislative, political channels or through the establishment of non-governmental interests and powers advocating lower inflation and increased central bank independence. It is thus important to realise that alternative, competing perspectives exist throughout almost all aspects of financial sector analysis. The approach taken in this study is to note and describe competing perspectives and their associated policy recommendations, while at the same time indicating which perspective/approach is likely to be best suited to a Vietnamese context.

In addition to consulting recent research on financial sector regulation in developing countries, particularly in Vietnam and South East Asia, the research group responsible for this study has employed the services of two local Vietnamese consultants, Le Khac Tri and Dang Nghiem Diem, who conducted background studies of the State Bank of Vietnam and the allocation of credit to the different sectors in the economy, respectively. The process of collecting and analysing data and writing the report was based on desk studies in Copenhagen and field trips to Vietnam. The latter has been of vital importance, as the opportunity to present and discuss ideas and perceptions resulted in new and more productive analyses. Preliminary findings and conclusions were presented at a number of meetings and a seminar held at the Central Institute for Economic Management in Hanoi in October 2002.

Numerous intellectual and creative debts are accumulated throughout the process of making a study of this nature. In this respect special thanks go to the president of the Central Institute of Economic Management (CIEM), Dr Dinh Van An, Vice-President Le Xuan Ba, and the director of the Nordic Institute of Asian Studies (NIAS), Dr Jorgen Delman. We are also grateful to World Bank staff, including economist Theo Ib Larsen and other colleagues at CIEM and NIAS. In addition, Dr Adam McCarthy and an anonymous referee have been very helpful in providing comments and suggestions for the revision. All errors and omissions remain, of course, the sole responsibility of the authors.

Introduction

This study is about the difficulties and problems encountered in the process of transforming the Vietnamese financial sector from one subordinate to government objectives and goals to an autonomous sector guided by market forces and competitive pressures.

Chapters 3 and 4 present a descriptive analysis of this process, making it evident that Vietnam has come a long way in changing its financial market from a centrally coordinated sector to a market economy. New markets and new institutions have been established and new legislation is in place. A gradual approach to reforms has abolished the more direct government control of the financial sector and reduced the still persistent indirect control. As a result, total credit intermediation by the banking sector now amounts to more than 40 per cent of GDP, considerably higher than in many other transitional economies.

The reform process has been gradual and has from time to time been set on the backburner for a period. This is not unusual. Evidence from other countries undergoing similar transitions testify that financial liberalisation and deregulation is a lengthy and difficult process occasionally involving setbacks and lack of real progress. A number of factors, however, suggest that the reform process is likely to be even more prolonged in the case of Vietnam. First, the French civil law tradition may slow down reforms. Second, and perhaps more important, the Vietnamese tradition of consensus governance in concert with the ruling elite's preference for social and political stability is also likely to act a brake on reforms. Third, the extensive links between the state-owned productive sector and the financial sector may also cause these reforms to take longer. Finally, the early crises in the process of liberalising the sector (most notably the collapse of the system of credit cooperatives) may also restrict the pace of reform. It may take a long time to rebuild trust in the formal financial market in turn causing newly established markets to take longer to develop. The fact that Vietnam was spared from the direct consequences of the East Asian Financial Crisis (EADC) suggests that the Vietnamese response to the crisis differed considerably from that of the other East Asian countries. While the latter strengthened and broadened reform efforts in response to the crisis, Vietnam imposed a temporary halt to comprehensive reforms – most likely to minimise the risk of social and political instability.

Although Vietnam has come a long way, considerable obstacles to financial sector liberalisation and deregulation remain. The persistence of policy-based lending is one such while the lack of transparency and accountability is another. As for the problem of non-performing loans in the banking sector, it is important to keep in mind that this problem in both the corporate and financial sectors also persists in most of the other East Asian countries affected by the EAFC. These countries have also embarked on a process of institutional reform, new banking and accounting standards, disclosure requirements and rules for corporate governance, but, as in Vietnam, the new rules and legislation that have been passed are not rigorously enforced.

Again, however, a number of factors combine to make it likely that the Vietnamese problems relating to non-performing loans will take even longer to resolve than in neighbouring countries. The first factor is the lack of transparency, as testified by the continued lack of international accounting estimates of the size of the NPL problem. The second factor is the culture of consensus governance blocking most attempts to reform the debt-ridden state-owned enterprises (SOEs). The third factor is that the banks holding the NPLs and the companies to whom these loans were given are both owned and controlled by the government, making it easier for the government to conceal the problem and/or to propose cosmetic solutions to it.

Following a descriptive analysis of the process of liberalising the financial sector, the study moves on to consider the progress already made from a regional perspective. More specifically, the analysis presented in Chapter 5 seeks to answer the question of how financial sector development, and more specifically banking sector supervision and regulation, in Vietnam compares to that found in neighbouring East Asian economies. Recognising that the level and character of supervision and regulation depends upon the level of competition in the sector, the analysis first compares the competitive pressure in the Vietnamese financial sector to that of its neighbours. Here it is found that although Vietnam in recent years has levelled the playing field for new entrants somewhat, there is still much to be done before the Vietnamese banking environment can be characterised as competitive or even partly competitive. Given that bank concentration in Vietnam coincides with state ownership, one option would be to strengthen the efforts to equitise the state-owned commercial banks (SOCBs). This is, however, a lengthy process that is unlikely to proceed unless the problems of non-performing loans and continued policy lending are resolved. Current thinking in Vietnam is that the equitisation of the SOCBs will not be piloted before 2006 at the earliest.

Another approach is to make financial markets more contestable – i.e. increase the competition between the banks already in the sector. Here, the signing of the Bilateral Trade Agreement with the United States stipulating a gradual opening of domestic financial markets to US banks ensures that this process will accelerate in the coming years. In this context, the concerns about the risk of 'unhealthy competition' among the SOCBs should be reconsidered. The Vietnamese banking sector is characterised by so little inter-bank competition that any indirect regulation – with the objective of making SOCBs 'stay within the areas assigned to them during the period of central planning' – is likely to make the eventual entry of foreign banks resemble shock therapy.

Any attempt to introduce new entrants and a higher level of competitiveness in the sector should of course be gradual so that the franchise value of local banks does not erode quickly, causing instability and increased risk of financial crises. As a consequence, any liberalisation of the entry process must be both managed over time and transparent. In addition, the regional comparison presented in Chapter 5 points to those areas where the Vietnamese government is most likely to benefit from strengthening the capacity and autonomy of the regulatory framework prior to opening the sector to foreign banks:

The promptness by which the regulator can or will respond to problems in the financial sector is generally lower in Vietnam than in the other countries in the region. Hence, while Vietnamese legislation is equal to or outperforms that of other countries of the region, the autonomy and power to rapidly implement these laws is lacking in Vietnam compared to those other countries.

Moreover, the Vietnamese banking system appears to be very restricted in respect of the types of activities banks can engage in. Banks in Vietnam are generally prohibited from operating in securities, insurance and real estate markets – activities that are permitted or only somewhat restricted in most other countries in the region. Finally, it was found that compared to the countries in the region Vietnam has very restrictive requirements regarding the amount of capital that a bank must have before being granted a permit to operate.

The institution responsible for the supervision and regulation of the financial sector in Vietnam is the State Bank of Vietnam (SBV). Consequently, Chapter 6 takes a closer look at SBV autonomy, SBV management of key financial markets and the measures taken to resolve the problem of NPLs burdening in particular the state-owned banks. Looking first at SBV autonomy, the overall conclusion is that the SBV cannot effectively develop and execute national monetary policies as long as it remains operationally and politically dependent upon support from other government agencies. The Vietnamese tradition of consensus governance thus appears to be in direct conflict with the conventional emphasis on creating autonomous central banks. This is likely to be the case whether one chooses to follow the direct (legislative) approach or the indirect (lobby-building) approach, although the expected increased presence of foreign banks is likely to increase the indirect pressure in the coming years.

In terms of the SBV role as a facilitator and organiser of financial markets, the current status of the market for government bonds and the inter-bank market for domestic and foreign currency are considered. Both markets appear to lack depth as well as breadth reflecting in part their early stage of development. The government moreover appears to have paid little attention to facilitating the development of a market-based benchmark yield curve, focusing solely on the fact that issuing bonds helps to finance budget deficits. In addition, a lack of coordination between the institutions issuing bonds (the SBV and the Ministry of Finance) in combination with a number of legislative restrictions restrict the growth of the secondary market for treasury bills. Conducting monetary policies through open market operations consequently seems to be too ambitious at the time of writing.

As for the role of the SBV as a supervisor and regulator of the financial markets and institutions, progress can be noted, although it is obvious that there is still a long way to go. This is particularly the case when it comes to adopting the international accounting and auditing practices which are likely to improve the overall transparency of the sector. In this context, the creation of a separate institution that is responsible for supervision and regulation could have the potential for further improvements in this area.

A number of problems related to judiciary, administrative and human capital related constraints are identified in relation to the measures taken to address the problem of NPLs. The limited autonomy and legal power associated with a system of decentralised asset management companies, in combination with the noted persistence of policy lending and a low stock of human capital, consequently make it highly unlikely that the recent progress in resolving NPLs can continue in the future.

Finally, Chapter 7 provides a brief description of how banks operate in the agricultural sector. This includes both the specific problems encountered by the different types of banks and their interrelation in the market. The focus on the agricultural sector in Chapter 7 rests upon the fact that the financial sector is the largest and most important in terms of employment and value of output. Here it is found that the government has in effect has laid down an explicit division of labour between the different financial institutions providing financial services to the rural population. In addition, the local communes, people's committees and mass organisations play a crucial role in the identification, screening and follow-up on clients for each type of institution. The result is that the initiatives to form joint-liability groups and/or contacts with potential lenders come from the institutions themselves. Overall, this reflects a top-down approach, which most likely originates in a desire to divide the market among the institutions in order to extend their outreach.

The competition and segmentation of the rural financial markets is further hampered by the widespread practice of offering subsidised interest rates. While this approach is chosen to improve development opportunities for the rural population, the net effects of this policy are likely to be negative and detrimental to the overall purpose of improving the livelihood of rural populations. In addition to restricting the mobilisation of savings, the practice of subsidising interest rates damages customer perception of credit, lowers the overall quality of financial services and reduces the quality of investment projects financed through the financial sector. All this runs counter to the government desire to develop and create growth opportunities for the agricultural sector.

Addressing these problems will involve profound structural changes in the rural financial sector. Long-term political commitment and allocation of resources is imperative. Failure to address either of these problems is, moreover, likely to affect adversely the efforts of the agricultural sector to remain competitive both nationally and internationally.

Overall, the analysis presented in this study supports the view that ensuring timely, fair and transparent supervision and regulation of the financial sector is of central importance to financial sector development and stability. Liberalising financial markets is thus not solely a question of limiting in many cases and/or restricting government influence. It might in fact involve the opposite since the influence and power of supervisory and regulatory institutions needs to be strengthened. As a consequence, the Vietnamese government will continue to play a central role for the financial sector, albeit it may be hoped through different channels of influence.

CHAPTER 1

Central planning and the first phase of reforms

THIS AND THE SUBSEQUENT CHAPTER will provide an overview of how the Vietnamese financial sector has evolved over time. The objective is in part to provide the background for the analyses presented in subsequent chapters, and in part to illustrate how the past continues to influence the present-day Vietnamese financial sector.

This chapter falls into three parts. The first section presents the institutional and historical background up to the beginning of the first comprehensive reforms in 1986, including the potential existence of a colonial legacy and events during the centrally co-ordinated economy established after independence. The second section describes events during the first phase of banking reforms and covers the period from 1986 to the East Asian Financial crisis (EAFC) in 1997. A descriptive analysis of the Vietnamese financial sector would, however, not be complete without some mention of the informal sector. Due to a dearth of data and information, it is not possible to describe the development of the informal sector over time. Instead, this chapter will end with a description of informal financial institutions to be found in Vietnam.

A descriptive analysis of events during the period after the EAFC up to the beginning of 2004 will be presented in the subsequent chapter. Overall, this second period can be characterised by a gradual increase in economic growth and a parallel gradual return to reforms. The period was initiated by the adoption of the Banking Law of 1998 stipulating the role and autonomy of the SBV and culminates with the announcement in 2001 of the restructuring and recapitalisation of the SOCBs.

THE COLONIAL LEGACY AND THE CENTRALLY COORDINATED ECONOMY

The idea that institutional transparency and accountability is dependent upon the legal, political and/or geographical endowments of a country has received a significant amount of attention over the last decade not least by the Bretton Woods institutions. The concern with institutional endowments as well as the efforts to change these are part and parcel of the 'second generation reforms' as presented by the IMF (Camdessus 1999). According to the IMF the focus of the 'first-generation reforms' was to make markets work more effectively through pricing, exchange-rate and interest-rate reforms parallel to tax and expenditure reforms and the establishment of rudimentary market institutions. The focus of second-generation reforms is to address the incentive structures that result from government bureaucracies and to develop the institutional capacity for reform: i.e. to get the institutions right.

In an East Asian context, the focus on institutions can, however, also be traced back to the EAFC, where a lack of institutional transparency and accountability was said by some observers to be a primary determinant of the crisis. This view reflected a body of opinion that argued that legal traditions, political structures and geographical endowments have a profound influence on a country's capacity for economic growth. For these reasons and in line with the historical perspective adopted in this chapter it makes sense to briefly review these factors with reference to Vietnam.

A recent World Bank study (Beck *et al.* 2001) evaluates the different theories of why some countries develop well-functioning financial systems. More specifically, why do some countries have laws that support financial development? Three theories/views on the historical determinants of financial development are assessed:

1. The legal view emphasising legal traditions as a central prerequisite for sound and stable financial sector development;

2. The political view rejecting the central role of the legal tradition and stressing instead the central influence of politics on financial sector development;

3. The endowment view emphasising the fact that geography and climate-induced disease proneness influence the formation of economic and political institutions and in turn financial sector development.

Turning first to the legal view, one can identify two primary channels through which legal tradition influences financial development: (a) legal traditions differ in terms of the priority they attach to private property rights and investor rights, and (b) the protection of these rights form the basis of financial contracting (La Porta *et al.* 1998 and 1999). If correct, one implication of this view is that historically determined differences in legal tradition can help to explain observed cross-country differences in financial development. According to the legal view, legal traditions are spread throughout the world through conquest, colonisation and imitation. Furthermore, once systems and institutions are in place, they are difficult to change and/or change very slowly. One implication is that a significant proportion of current international differences in financial development can be traced to different historical origins and traditions dating back to the colonial era in less-developed countries.

Table 1.1 contains a listing of the legal origins of some of the South East Asian countries. Vietnam and Cambodia are the only countries with a legal environment that is influenced by both Socialist and a French legal tradition. One of the main conclusions in La Porta *et al.* (1998, 1999) is that countries with a French civil law tradition appear to be less effective in supporting financial development than countries with a German, British or Scandinavian legal tradition/system. The explanation provided by La Porta *et al.* is that French civil law is more static than, for example, common law systems like the British.

More specifically, a common law tradition is argued to be a better source of and predictor for rule of law, transparency and accountability. A civil law tradition, on the other hand, is argued to be more prone to privilege state intervention in economic processes and to be less sensitive to concerns about the rule of law and transparency. In addition, a civil law tradition is argued to be associated with a widespread distrust of judges, distaste for jurisprudence and for having open judicial disputations. Countries with a French legal tradition are thus more comfortable with rigid bright-line rules and legal certainty. This in turn implies that countries with a French legal tradition are likely to be less responsive towards sectors and conditions that change frequently (as is often the case with the financial sector). In short, the financial sector will typically not be facing a sufficiently high level of judicial discretion in countries with a French legal tradition. This in turn is likely to have a detrimental effect upon financial sector development.

The importance of legal traditions has, however, been disputed. One example is Woo-Cumings (2001) who argues that legal traditions and institutions do not determine the nature of the state in East Asia. According to Woo-Cumings, the studies stressing the importance of institutions reflect an anti-state bias. Furthermore, Woo-Cumings argues that governance structures are much too complicated to be reduced to a question of the type of legal system.

If one, however, chooses to accept the idea that legal origin does matter, as proposed by (among others) La Porta *et al.*, the policy implications are quite clear. While Vietnam cannot change its legal origin, it can – albeit with considerable effort – reform its judicial system. This could take the form of emphasising the rights of outside investors by making contract enforcement more efficient, and by creating a legal system that more effectively evolves to support changing economic conditions. Yet another implication of accepting the idea that legal origin is important is that Vietnam should be careful about making direct inferences and/or adopting Chinese financial development policies without prior modifications and adaptation according to a Vietnamese context. The reason is the different legal origin. The policies necessary in order to secure sound financial development in Vietnam may be much more fundamental and far-reaching than those implemented in China.

Turning next to the so-called political view of financial development, this theory predicts that political factors will dominate the legal factors in determining the level and/or pace of financial sector development. These theories are inspired by North (1990) and Olson (1993). The argument is that the elites will pursue their own interests through government policies. Furthermore, the proponents of the political view stress that political structures inherently tend to thwart financial development. It can, for example, be argued that a centralised and powerful government tends to be incompatible with financial development. The underlying reasoning is that the proper functioning of financial institutions and markets requires imposing limitations on government discretion. These limits can, however, be incompatible with the ambitions of a centralised and powerful state. The elite will only press for laws and institutions that stimulate financial development if it views itself as being enriched and more secure by free, competitive financial markets.

According to the Legislative and Executive Index of Political Competitiveness (LEIPC) depicted in Table 1.1, one might predict difficulties in developing a sound and well-functioning financial system in Vietnam, China and Indonesia as all three countries are characterised by a non-competitive political environment.[1]

Any prediction on the importance of a non-competitive political environment should, however, be contrasted with the results of Beck *et al.* (2001), who find that measures of the initial and current political structure do not explain cross-country variations in financial development. Hence, empirical analysis does not support the notion of political structure shaping financial develop ment. As a consequence, the implications of a low LEIPC financial develop-ment score should stand alone but be supported by additional evidence before stressing the point further.

Finally, according to the 'endowment view' it is argued that differences in geography and disease proneness have shaped patterns of political, institutional, and economic development. Gallup *et al.* (1998) find that geographical position influences the types of diseases that exist and the organisation of economic activity. This in turn it is argued influence the formation of institutions, political arrangements and the level and pace of economic development.

According to this line of research, areas with poor agriculture and areas that are geographically isolated cannot exploit economies of scale in agriculture, restricting their ability to create broad-based economic growth. In addition, countries dominated by 'poor' climate have a correspondingly lower probability of developing the political, legal, and institutional foundations that support complex and specialised economic interactions restricting long-run economic growth.

Table 1.1: Legal origin, political system and initial endowments

	Legal origin	LEIPC *	Latitude (mean = 0.26)	Tropical climate (mean = 0.60)	Log settler mortality (mean = 4.66)
Vietnam	French/ Socialist	8	0.18	Yes (1)	4.94
Cambodia	French/ Socialist	12	0.14	Yes (1)	n.a.
China	German/ Socialist	6	0.39	No (0)	n.a.
Indonesia	French	8	0.06	Yes (1)	5.14
Korea	German	14	0.41	No (0)	n.a.
Malaysia	British	14	0.03	Yes (1)	2.89
Philippines	French	14	0.14	Yes (1)	n.a.
Thailand	British	14	0.17	Yes (1)	n.a.

Sources: La Porta et al. (1998, 1999), Beck et al. (2001); Database of Political Institutions (DPI), see Beck et al. (2000), Acemoglu et al. (2001); Global Development Network Database, see www.worldbank.org/research/growth/

*Note: Legislative and executive index of political competitiveness (LEIPC) ranges from 2 to 14. A score of 2 indicates a non-competitive political environment, while a score of 14 indicates the most competitive political system. The data presented are for the year 1997.

The endowment view therefore predicts that countries in poor geographical and disease environments will have less well-developed financial institutions than countries with better initial endowments. Acemoglu et al. (2001) focus on the disease environment, and argue that the initial disease environment was decisive in whether colonisers created a 'settler' or an 'extractive' colony. If the colonisers encountered a hostile (i.e. high mortality) setting, they would choose to develop institutions that were extractive – i.e. designed to capture an already existing surplus for the colonial power. If, on the other hand, the environment was not too hostile to the first settlers (i.e. a low mortality setting), the colonial powers would choose to create institutions that could further develop the country for the benefit of the colonial power.

As a consequence, the early environment faced by the first settlers is likely to have had decisive influence upon the types of institutions and modes of operation left by the colonial powers. If one furthermore believes that formal and informal institutional change only occurs very slowly and with great effort, the colonial heritage is likely to still have an influence on current institutions and practices. Thus, according to the endowment view, the initial conditions continue to exert a profound influence on the present day financial sector. Consequently, a better knowledge of these factors will assist in predicting whether or not countries in poor geographical and disease environments have less well-developed financial institutions.

Looking again at Table 1.1, three indicators of initial endowments are listed. The first two, latitude of capital in the respective countries and the World Bank classification of whether or not a country has a tropical climate, indicate that Vietnam from an endowment point of view is no worse off than the rest of the region. Only China and Korea are considered not to have a tropical climate. In addition, the latitude of their respective capitals is the highest among the countries considered here. Looking at the third indicator, settler mortality, Vietnam does not deviate much from the sample mean of an average annual total of 140 casualties among every thousand soldiers.[2] Hence, there is nothing that indicates that Vietnam should be worse off than any other country in the South East Asian region when it comes to institutional determinants and structure when evaluated from an endowments point of view.

Beck *et al.* (2001) evaluate the power of all three theories (the legal, the political and the endowment view) to explain the level of financial development. The results appear to be most in line with the 'legal view'. Differences in legal origin can thus help explain the development of financial institutions today, even after controlling for a number of other determinants of economic growth.[3] With this result in mind it would appear the legal origin represents a key challenge in the ongoing efforts to reform and develop the Vietnamese financial sector. The question of the role of the non-competitive political system will be analysed in more detail below.

Having looked at the historically set institutional determinants of the Vietnamese financial system, we now turn to look at events in the period after the French colonisation. Even prior to the end of the French colonisation, the Second National Party Congress held in 1951 in Tuyen Quang established a national bank, the State Bank of Vietnam (the SBV). This was as part of the infrastructure put in place in the Northern provinces controlled by the Viet Minh. From 1951 to 1954, the main duties of the SBV encompassed financial transactions and a rudimentary set of central bank functions. These included the control of the issuance of banknotes as well as of monetary circulation, the management of the state treasury, the management and control of foreign exchange and money transactions and the mobilisation of funds and the provision of loans for production and commodity circulation. During this period the Office of State Inspection audited the activities of the SBV.

In 1954 after the French colonial period and the partition of the country, all financial institutions were nationalised and merged with the SBV. Banking activities during this period were directed towards supporting construction in the North and the war in the South. Upon unification in 1975, all financial institutions in the South were also nationalised and merged with the SBV. Banking activities were subsequently redirected to restore the economy and to develop the country as a whole. A centrally coordinated system was applied to the economy as well as to the banking system.

During the period 1976–89 Vietnam had a one-tier nation-wide banking system owned and controlled by the state. Hence, the SBV acted both as a central bank and as a commercial bank for the government. As a consequence a monetary market did not develop and commercial banks did not exist in the full sense. The financial system was reduced to being an instrument for executing government policies, continuously accommodating the needs of the state budget and the state-owned enterprises (the SOEs). The regime of directed and subsidised credit resulted in negative real interest rates, and interest rates on deposits were higher than interest rates on loans (interest rate inversion).

According to Rana and Hamid (1995) the government paid little attention to monetary issues during this period. In addition, as pointed out by McCarthy (2001), neither the government nor the omnipresent Vietnamese Communist Party (VCP) exercised a tight control over all types of activities in the economy. In the words of McCarthy (2001) the VCP was 'above and inside all organised activity, but only intervenes when it feels threatened. The interplay of interest groups is therefore allowed within this framework without permitting discrete points of authority to stand out', and van Donge *et al.* (1999) has consequently characterised the method of rule employed by the VCP as 'a system of checks and balances operating around the principle of consensus'.

This description of the Vietnamese culture of governance is confirmed by Appold and Phong (2001) who describe central planning committees and ministries as 'locuses of negotiation and bargaining between the state and its economic agents, the state owned enterprises'. Hence, even if one could obtain a full insight into past and present central decision-making processes, they are not likely to reveal detailed plans stipulating, for example, the terms and conditions for the allocation of credit. The fact that credible information has been (and still is) both scattered and sparse only adds to the difficulties involved with getting an accurate assessment of the nature and degree of direct government control of the Vietnamese financial sector. Accordingly, any assessment of this nature can only be tentative, relying on indirect measures and the detection of indicative patterns.

In 1958 the Vietnamese Bank for Investment and Development (VBID) was established as a specialised bank responsible for the financing of large (primarily infrastructural) investments for SOEs. Five years later in 1963 another bank, the Bank for Foreign Trade (Vietcombank), was established to handle all financial transactions relating to foreign trade. Both specialised banks were fully owned by the government and operated as a special department of the SBV, essentially maintaining the one-tier banking system.

The restrictions placed on SBV operations and the redundant nature of this type of centrally controlled monetary policy, however, made financial and monetary conditions difficult. The results were over-expenditure of the state budget, hyperinflation and serious macroeconomic unbalances. The government attempted to remedy the problems by carrying out currency reforms in 1976, 1979 and 1985 (Klump and Gottwald, 2003). These all failed, leading inflation to reach hyperinflationary levels (775 per cent in early 1986).

INITIATING TRANSITION: THE FIRST PHASE OF REFORMS, 1986–97

Facing the above mentioned severe economic imbalances, the Sixth Communist Congress, held in December 1986, was characterised by a sense of crisis and self-criticism over the party's failure to improve the economy. It was imperative that the government did something. Past failures to resolve the crisis in concert with the fact that the government had to act implied that the government was open to experiments and that the normal emphasis on establishing consensus was a second-order priority. Consequently, the Sixth Communist Congress ended with a decision to launch a comprehensive reform policy. These reforms, labelled 'Doi Moi' (renovation), initiated the transition from a centrally planned to a more market-orientated economy. There had been earlier attempts to loosen government control – most notably the decollectivisation process in the agricultural sector had been initiated in 1981. The Doi Moi reforms were, however, the first systematic reforms aimed at transforming a system previously based on administrative subsidies into one of independence and self-support – in short – to loosen government control over the economy.

The Doi Moi reforms had important implications for the Vietnamese economy. The year 1989 witnessed the initiation of the processes of decollectivisation and privatisations in the agricultural sector, making this sector the first to see a rapid growth in private enterprises. Reforms of the price and rationing systems were carried out as compensations for losses when price controls were abolished. In addition, the exchange rate was unified and devalued five times. The initial round of reforms also contained a significant element of anti-inflationary policies, including sharp increases in the interest rate and limits to credit expansion. As a result inflation fell markedly from triple digits as experienced in the 1980s to single-digit rates towards the end of the first period (see Figure 1.1).

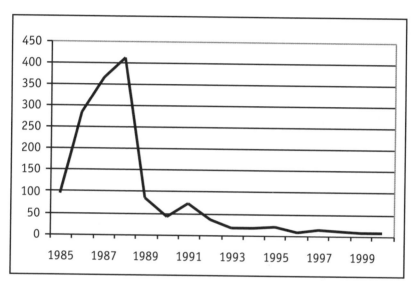

Figure 1.1: Inflation (annual GDP deflator)
Source: WDI (2002)

The fall in inflation was followed by a parallel fall in interest rates, resulting in positive real interest rates and the end of interest rate inversion (deposit rates being higher than lending rates). In addition, the Doi Moi reforms meant that the government implemented a number of measures intended to reduce the overall fiscal deficit through the elimination of budget subsidies, the reduction of credit to state enterprises and measures to streamline the bureaucracy.

In the financial sector the reform process was initiated by the following two key decisions:

1. On 3 July 1987, the chairman of the Council of Ministers (the prime minister) issued Decision 218/CT to transform the state-owned banks into commercial banks;

2. On 26 March 1988, the chairman of the Council of Ministers signed Decree No.53/ND on shifting the one-tier banking system towards a business-orientated structure thereby establishing state-owned, specialised commercial banks that were separate from the SBV.

The above mentioned Decree 53 was the first step towards transforming the one-tier banking system into a two-tier system, but in reality state management and business duties still overlapped.

In May 1990, the promulgation of two ordinances on banking established for the first time the objectives, duties and operation purposes for each tier of the banking system. The first, the Law for the Vietnamese Central Bank, confirmed the shift to a two-tiered banking system. The SBV was officially made responsible for state management of the banking system and given the duties of a central bank. These included stabilising the value of the currency, securing the safety and stability of the banking system and promoting the development of the economy (see Chapter 4). The already existing two state-owned banks operating under the auspices of the SBV (the VBID and the Vietcombank) were transformed into to state-owned commercial banks, while two new SOCBs, the Vietnam Industrial and Commercial Bank (the Incombank) and the Bank for Agriculture and Rural Development (VBARD) were created in 1991. The SOCBs were made responsible for the operation and control of their finances as well as the implementation of universal banking activities in their respective spheres.[4]

In addition to confirming the autonomy of the SOCBs, the second law – the National Law on Banks – also allowed for the establishment of private commercial banks and, to a lesser degree, branch offices and representative offices of foreign banks. The domestic commercial banks permitted were joint-stock banks (JSB),[5] joint-venture banks (JVBs) between the government and foreign financial institutions and credit cooperatives (CC). Table 1.2 outlines the subsequent growth in second-tier banking institutions.

Table 1.2: Commercial banks (units)

	1991	1992	1993	1994	1995	1996	1997	1998	1999
Urban joint-stock banks	4	16	25	29	29	31	31	31	28
Rural joint-stock banks	0	6	16	16	19	20	20	20	20
Joint-venture banks	1	2	3	3	4	4	4	4	5
Foreign banks	0	5	8	9	18	22	24	25	26

Source: Department of Banks, State Bank of Vietnam

In short, the two ordinances on banks promulgated in 1990 formalised the separation of financial and business operations from the organisational structure of the state bank. As such the ordinances represent an important stage of progress in the banking industry, whereby commercial banking and the organisational practice of private enterprises were formally disengaged from that of the ministries concentrating on state management functions.

The issuance of the two Ordinances in 1990 represented a turning point for the SBV. It was defined to be separate a government institution with legal capital. In addition, the placement of the SBV headquarters in Hanoi was reaffirmed. Moreover, given that implementing financial transactions were no longer part of the SBV remits the new law resulted in significant internal reorganisations in the SBV. Staff were replaced and transferred to the SOCBs in order to fit with the new functions, tasks and organisational structure. More specifically, one division was transferred to state-owned commercial banks, while the rest were placed in departments of the SBV concentrating on developing and executing national monetary policies, managing business operations of credit institutions and studying proposals and drafts determining regulations and the legal basis for managing monetary business and the banking operations of credit institutions and non-banking financial institutions. Other departments such as the policy study department, the foreign exchange management department and the international relations department remained in the organisational structure of the SBV (see Chapter 4).

Overall, financial sector reforms in many cases preceded reforms in the real sector – most notably the SOE sector, a sequencing of reforms that probably had adverse consequences for the subsequent success of the overall reforms. In general, the economic literature on economic liberalisation and the sequencing of reforms in developing countries is vast and non-unified. It is consequently difficult to derive clear, undisputable policy implications. However, one policy recommendation that emerges quite generally and despite the aforementioned difficulties is that the liberalisation of the domestic real sector should precede the liberalisation of the domestic financial sector (Johnston 1994). A financial sector guided by market principles will find it difficult (if not impossible) to evaluate the profitability of different client sectors and/or firms for whom they wish to provide credit if relative prices in a non-liberalised real sector are distorted (or perhaps missing).[6]

While it is difficult to trace and/or estimate the precise implications of this divergence from the recommended sequencing of reforms, it is important to point out that the Vietnamese banks are still struggling with the lack of transparency and market incentives that continue to characterise the only partly liberalised SOE sectors. One can therefore point to the initial sequence of reforms as one of the structural aspects of the past that continues to exert considerable influence on financial sector performance.

Another general finding that emerges from other studies of economic liberalisation in developing countries is that any transformation of a state-controlled monobank system into a diversified market-based financial system is a lengthy and laborious process. Vietnam is no exception. Despite the creation and entry of a large number of new banks, the dominance of the government-controlled banks was not reduced significantly over the period. A notable exception was, however, the resurgence of the credit cooperative

(CC) system. As the rapid growth, and even faster demise, of the CC system is likely to have had lasting and very important implications for the Vietnamese financial system, it is useful to elaborate on the chain of events.

By the time the number of CCs began to grow rapidly in the mid-1980s they were already well-known financial institutions in Vietnam. The first credit cooperatives were established in North Vietnam in 1956, and they numbered 5,500 in the early 1960s. By 1983 the first CCs were established in South Vietnam, and their number continued to grow rapidly during the mid-1980s. By the end of the decade their number stood at 7,180. The credit cooperatives of this epoch were operating in isolation in small communities beyond the reach of the SBV. Often the sole source of funding in the local area, the practice of operating in isolated communities was continued in the initial round of financial sector reforms, No automatic refinancing mechanism by the SBV was consequently ensured prior to the rapid growth of the CC system. Some re-financing by the SBV was available, but it was neither automatic nor predictable.

As a result of the above mentioned initial wave of privatisations in the agricultural sector, the demand for credit from this sector soared. The VBARD, however, served only agricultural SOEs (Le Roy and Robert 1999), causing private enterprises and farmers to turn to the CC system in order to obtain credit. The result was a very rapid growth of CCs credit cooperatives in the rural areas. In order to meet the demand for credit some of the CCs tried to attract local savings by offering very attractive rates sometimes up to 15 per cent per month (Fforde and De Vylder, 1996). Unfortunately, the staffs in charge were often poorly trained, and a number of cases of fraudulent behaviour were reported. Early during 1990 the first credit cooperatives began to encounter problems. As refinancing by the SBV was insufficient, a number of CCs had to close as government subsidies dried up. With arrears mounting depositors panicked and rushed to withdraw their money, triggering a run on CCs throughout the country.

The effect on the CC system was disastrous. The lack of re-financing facilities, back-up funds and deposit insurance virtually ensured that the majority (over 7,000) of the isolated credit co-operatives would become bankrupt. By the end of 1990 only 160 credit cooperatives were operational, the rest had had to close due to mounting arrears. The consequences for the agricultural sector were devastating. In addition to the numerous agricultural households that lost their savings, the collapse of the credit cooperatives also affected newly established small and medium-sized enterprises (SMEs) who had used the CCs as a key source of credit. It is estimated that the crisis caused more than 2,000 small enterprises to go bankrupt (Fforde and De Vylder 1996).

The government reacted to the crisis in the CC system by strengthening SBV monitoring and by granting more autonomy to the SOCBs to create a more competitive environment. These measures were primarily designed to prevent the spread of the crisis, while little was done to amend the damages caused directly by the collapse of the CC system. The major long-term effect, however, appears to have been psychological. The collapse of the credit cooperatives severely undermined the general faith and confidence in the formal financial system.

The government attempted to fill the financing gap caused by the virtual disappearance of the credit cooperative system. The newly formed VBARD was strengthened and by decree no. 202 of 6 August 1991 given the task of lending directly to peasant families. The VBARD could not, however, fill the void from the collapsed rural credit cooperatives.[7] The government subsequently entrusted the SBV with the creation and organisation of an entirely new (replacement) network of local credit windows.[8] As the primary objective was to re-establish confidence in the financial sector, the name 'cooperative' was also replaced by 'People's Credit Funds' (PCFs). After a study of the options available in several countries, the government of Vietnam chose to adapt the Canadian Desjardins' model to a Vietnamese context.

The result was a hierarchical organisation with three management levels. Local Credit Funds (LCFs) supplied households and SMEs with financial services while being handled and directed by a Regional Credit Fund (RCF). The RCFs would in turn be supervised by a Central Credit Fund (CCF) handling the supply and balancing of liquidity among the RFCs. If the distance from a LCF to a RCF was too great the LCF was managed directly by the SBV. It was, however, the plan that each LCF should be associated with a RCF. According to Wolff (1999) there were 950 LCFs at the end of the 1990s.

The choice of a three-layer organisation was thus intended to achieve the combination of close local contacts and connections while minimising the risks associated with seasonality and regional shocks – problems that are especially pertinent in rural areas where the sources of income are subject to the same shocks.

While the intention was that the PCF system should be developed from both above (the SBV) and below (the founding members identified with the help of the local people's committee), this was not the case in practice. Most initiatives to start up new LCFs came from the SBV. In addition, as pointed out by Rana and Hamid (1995), LCF staffs often lacked banking training and technical equipment. As a consequence, the SBV provided intensive support in the control, supervision and training of staff, in particular during the implementation stage.

Consequently, the events during this first phase of reforms did little to curb government dominance over the financial sector. The SOCBs continued to dominate the financial sector and the PCF system was (as mentioned above) not an independent, non-governmental alternative. As for the joint-venture banks, they were all 50:50 joint ventures between SOCBs and foreign banks from neighbouring countries,[9] indicating that they were also not free from government control. The majority of their business is furthermore related to trade financing with the home country of the foreign counterpart (i.e. Indonesia, Malaysia, Korea and Thailand). The only domestic private-sector involvement in the formal financial sector was among the JSBs and even here some of them were jointly owned by SOEs, private groups and individuals. Others were, however, 100 per cent owned by private investors.[10]

Finally, there were, of course, the foreign banks. Here, the events following the opening of the Vietnamese market can best be described as one of initial optimism followed by a gradual cooling. As depicted in Table 1.2, the number of foreign banks in Vietnam rose rapidly to 22 in 1995 only to remain at this level until the end of the period.

While the initial expectation was that Vietnam would be a booming and attractive East Asian market along the lines of Korea and Thailand was fulfilled, the foreign banks had to operate under restrictive regulations. Foreign banks were, for example, only given licenses for 20 years. They were allowed to take dong deposits but only up to an equivalent of US$ 1.5 million, and they were only allowed to lend a maximum of 10 per cent of their capital to a single borrower (Ninh 2003), leaving the foreign banks were left with trade financing, the provision of letters of credit for import and export (mostly for foreign firms), and the processing of remittances. Due to the number of foreign banks operating in Vietnam, such activities were associated with low profits and high risks (Klump and Gottwald 2003).[11]

The persistent dominance of government-controlled financial institutions implied a continuation of an intimate relationship between the SOCBs and the state-owned enterprises. Figure 1.2 shows that although the ratio of credit to the private sector increased from 10 per cent in 1990 to just below 30 per cent in 1998, the SOEs still received the major part of bank credit throughout the period.

As depicted in Table 1.3, a similar pattern is found when looking at the ratio of credit in foreign currency. Table 1.3 also shows that the overall increase in the share of foreign-currency credit allocated to the private sector is not universal across the different entities that make up the private sector. While credit to joint ventures and foreign-invested companies has almost quadrupled over the relatively short period, the share of credit allocated to individuals and households has been reduced to below a third of its 1994 level. Moreover, although the proportion of banking credit to the private sector has increased considerably from 1990, Table 1.4 shows that the SOCB share of state and non-state credit differs substantially from that of the JSBs. This suggests that some degree of exclusion of private enterprises was taking place.

The intimate relationship between the SOCBs and the SOE sector is likely to have had a detrimental effect upon the strength

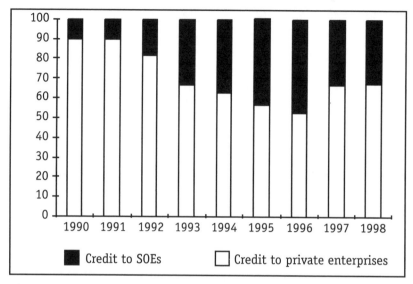

Figure 1.2: Credit to SOEs and private enterprises
Source: IMF (1999)

Table 1.3: Foreign currency credit to state and non-state enterprises (per cent)

	1994	1995	1996	1997	1998
SOEs	81.7	76.3	75.8	78.8	72.2
Private sector	18.3	23.7	24.2	21.2	27.8
Of which:					
Cooperatives	0.2	0.2	0.3	0.1	0.1
Shareholding and limited liability companies	7.7	9.8	7.4	12.1	10.8
Joint-venture and foreign-invested companies	4.7	11.4	14.5	17.1	15.0
Individuals, households	6.2	2.2	2.0	1.9	1.9

Source: IMF (1999)

Table 1.4: Lending to non-state institutions (per cent share of total lending)

	1994	1995	1996	1997	1998
JSB lending	58.2	62.6	61.5	67.5	71.4
SOCB lending	32.6	74.0	42.5	44.6	42.1

Source: IMF (1999)

of the banking sector through several channels. First, the SOE sector was characterised by low efficiency and resulting difficulties in servicing their debts. This caused a deterioration of SOCB balance sheets especially. According to official statistics from the SBV, the SOCBs held 75 per cent of total overdue loans in 1997. It is, however, likely that the official figures underestimate the magnitude of the problem since ever-greening (rolling over overdue loans into new loans) of in particular SOE loans was both allowed and widely practised. In addition, loan classification in Vietnam did not follow international practices and definitions. For example, instead of classifying an entire loan as non-performing in the case of defaulting payments, the approach according to Vietnamese accounting standards was to classify only the actual arrears as non-performing while classifying the remainder of the principal as still active and per-forming. Hence, even if the practice of ever-greening is limited, it is clear that this accounting practice will result in estimates of non-performing loans that are much lower than they would have been had international accounting standards been applied. The problem of the non-performing loans in the SOCBs and the recent measures to resolve these are discussed in depth in Chapter 4.

Second, and directly related to the above-mentioned problems, is the fact that the SOCB loans to SOEs were concentrated within certain sectors. This implies that risk exposure for these banks was (and remains) very high. In addition, the practice of providing un-secured loans and having non-standard and non-transparent provisioning rules further aggravated the problem. As a result bank viability and financial sector stability is crucially dependent upon how the non-performing loan problem is resolved. Third, the exten-sive direct government control of credit allocation means that staff skills and knowledge of creditor screening and supervision became superfluous. As a consequence, specialised staff skills and knowledge about, for example, loan assessment and provisioning was not generated and/or maintained in the state-controlled banks.

These problems in the banking sector were already apparent during the first period (1986–97). However, the close relationship between the Vietnamese banking and SOE sectors in combination with the government emphasis on social stability meant that any attempt to tackle the banking problems was crucially dependent on the health of the SOEs. The Vietnamese government could not accept a situation where banks, following a banking sector reform, refused to extend credit to non-reformed SOEs since a likely result would be financial problems and massive layouts in the SOE sector that in turn could jeopardise the social and political stability of the country. The significance attached to maintaining social stability and the implications for the limited latitude for financial sector reforms were to become even more evident in the period following the East Asian Financial Crisis in 1997. Despite the fact that such problems became visible during the first phase (1986–97) the economy overall reacted positively to the Doi Moi reforms. As depicted in Figure 1.3 annual GDP growth almost doubled from a level around 5.1 per cent in 1990 to 9.5 per cent in the peak year of 1995.

Towards the end of the period economic growth and the reform process began to stall. Possible reasons for this slowdown in GDP growth are manifold: ranging from problems of moral hazard and lack of incentives in the state-owned enterprises to endemic corruption and an inflexible bureaucracy. In addition, the country was hit by the worst tropical storm in 50 years and widespread peasant unrest in the northern province of Thai Binh during 1997. Both factors undoubtedly contributed a general loss of confidence in both economic policies and opportunities. The result was a visible deceleration of the economy. Hence, the first signs of vulnerability became visible prior to the severe regional financial crisis waiting in the wings.

The drop in GDP growth rates was, however, not the sole negative development during the first period. The crisis in the

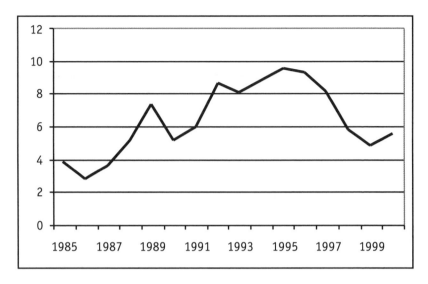

Figure 1.3: Annual GDP growth (per cent)
Source: WDI (2002)

private credit cooperatives, coupled with a history of government control and lack of transparency, provides a possible explanation for the comparatively low mobilisation of savings via the formal financial sector as depicted in Figure 1.4.

As the figure shows, the ratio of gross domestic savings to GDP rose rapidly in the beginning of the reform period – most likely due to the drop in inflation rates and renewed confidence in the reform process. The growth of gross domestic savings did not, however, continue and remained below 20 per cent until end of the first period in 1997. This compares poorly to neighbouring countries like the China (gross domestic savings around 42–43 per cent of GDP) and Thailand (gross domestic savings between 31–35 per cent of GDP).

The limited trust in formal financial institutions resulting from the collapse of the CC system is likely to have played a key role in explaining the failure to further increase the ratio of savings to GDP as the low confidence in formal financial institutions caused many to withdraw or abstain from channelling their funds to the

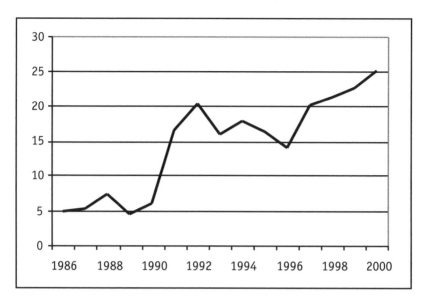

Figure 1.4: Gross domestic savings (per cent of GDP)
Source: WDI (2002)

banks and to buy gold and dollars instead. According to Klump and Gottwald (2003) several institutional changes combined to make it easier and more attractive for both households and companies to hold US$ during this period. First, the legal ban on holding dollars was lifted in 1988, and three years later in 1991 domestic banks were allowed to offer time deposits denominated in foreign currency. Second, the collapse of the Soviet Union in 1989 caused the rouble-based trade with former Eastern bloc countries to be replaced by trade and foreign direct investments in dollars. Third, the devaluation of the dong in 1989 led savers to expect future devaluations. This factor in turn implied that dollars were preferred to dong when it came to safeguarding currency holdings and savings. As a consequence, both the medium of exchange motive[12] and the store of value motive[13] are likely to have played a role in the growing circulation of dollars in Vietnam.

The problems associated with a high degree of dollarisation are twofold. First, the existence of a parallel currency system will make it more difficult for a government to conduct monetary policy as shifts in demand and supply of dollars are difficult to predict let alone control.[14] Second, the use of dollars will undermine the revenue the government derives from seignorage[15] and the implicit inflation tax imposed on holders of domestic currency.[16] As a consequence, governments have frequently sought to limit or prohibit the use and holding of dollars. This in turn has made the phenomenon very difficult to track and measure. Vietnam is no exception, and no estimate of the precise amount of dollars circulating in the Vietnamese economy exists. According to Freeman (1998) the official estimate of the amount of dollars was 600 million in 1997, but unofficial sources put the figure at around 3 billion. The large remittances flowing in through both official[17] and unofficial channels and the increase in the ratio of foreign currency loans to total loans are, however, likely to have increased this amount significantly since then.

The lack of precise estimates of the ratio of legitimate foreign currency deposits to total deposits or M2 is often used as a proxy for the degree of dollarisation. The underlying assumption behind this choice of proxy variable is that although the ratio of foreign currency deposits probably does not reflect the level of dollarisation it might give an indication of the trend and movements in the degree of dollarisation.

According to Leung and Huy Duc (1999), there were no significant holdings of dollars in the country in the decade prior to 1985.[18] This, however, started to change as the barter trade with the Soviet Union decreased and domestic inflation accelerated from 1986 (see Figure 1.2), leading to increased demand for US$.

Looking at Figure 1.5 it can be seen that foreign currency deposits increased dramatically in the beginning of the period. They then declined towards the end of the first period of reforms in 1997, only to rise again in recent years. Unteroberdoerster (2002) argues that the 'medium of exchange motive' is the most likely explanation for the rapid rise in foreign currency deposits in the early 1990s. As for the increase in foreign currency deposits from 1996, Unteroberdoerster (2002) points to the 'store of value motive' as the most likely explanation. This is due to the fact that inflation was under control in this period (see Figure 1.2) and that the EAFC,

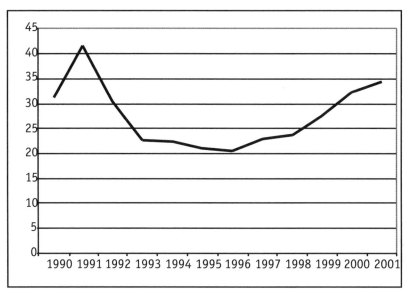

Figure 1.5: Foreign currency deposits (per cent of M2)

Source: Unteroberdoerster (2002)

in combination with lower economic growth, made agents uncertain of the government's will and capacity to defend the exchange rate.

Finally, Unteroberdoerster (2002) suggests that the recent increase in dollarisation appears to have been caused by a combination of asset substitution and increased integration with the global economy.[19] As can be seen from Figure 1.5, the increase in dollarisation and the overall decline in economic activity (see Figure 1.3), began prior to the EAFC. Both developments reflect that the Vietnamese economy was already in crisis by the time the East Asian Financial Crisis occurred.

INFORMAL FINANCIAL INSTITUTIONS

Although still scattered and sparse, information about the informal financial markets and institutions in Vietnam has improved since 1989 as the gradually increased reliance on market forces has resulted in a parallel rise in the recognition of the importance of the informal financial sector. The unregulated and at times illegal activities taking place in this sector, however, still imply that neither comprehensive nor fully reliable data exist on the magnitude and character of the informal sector. The following informal credit institutions are considered in turn: moneylenders, Roscas, loans from relatives and friends and trader credit.

Generally, moneylenders are wealthy individuals who lend their own funds and/or funds borrowed from other sources. Their clients are households who need short-term capital for production purposes and poor households who need money to cope with emergencies. The necessary procedures for obtaining a loan are very simple, usually just a piece of paper stipulating the contract agreed upon by money-lender and the client. In some cases, no paper exists, so the parties rely on oral agreements.

Loans can be made in both cash and kind, and the specific terms of the contract such as interest rate and duration depend on the relationship between lender and borrower. Overall, if the loan has been in cash, surveys have found that the interest rate level is between two to five times higher than that of formal credit. The duration of the loan is typically short, measured in weeks or months and only rarely exceeding a full year. The loans in kind are especially popular in rural areas, where a poor household is provided with foodstuff or seed by the lender, who in turns demands a repayment in cash or rice.

Rotating Savings and Credit Associations (Roscas) are found in almost all regions of the world. A Rosca usually consists of a group of people who are voluntarily or involuntarily excluded from the formal financial system. The group meets on a regular basis all bringing a pre-determined amount, which is subsequently put into a Rosca pool. Through recurrent meetings this pool is sequentially allocated once to every group member. After having received the pool, members have to continue to contribute to the Rosca until every member has received it once.

The objectives of a Rosca are often twofold: (i) to obtain economies of scale by pooling the collective savings of the group, and (ii) to provide external incentives to save through the obligation to the Rosca group. This second motive is intrinsically linked to issues of intra-household allocation of resources since the majority of Roscas are typically all-female groups. The primary advantage of joining a Rosca is that all but one member (the one who receives the pool in the last round) will obtain funds faster than if she had chosen to save on her own. The primary challenges facing Rosca participants are likewise twofold: (i) to ensure member compliance such that they continue to contribute to the Rosca after having received the pool, and (ii) to determine how to allocate the pool in each round.

While Rosca members usually rely on a combination of an informal sanctions/reputation effect and the limited mobility of Rosca members to deal with the problem of compliance, the problem of allocating the pool is essentially a choice among different types of Roscas. They include: (i) a random Rosca (where the pool is allocated through a lottery among the eligible members – i.e. those who have yet to receive the pool); (ii) a bidding Rosca (where the pool is allocated through sequential auctions in which each eligible member states the maximum reduction in the contribution from the other eligible members that she is prepared to accept); and (iii) a discrete Rosca (where the pool is allocated according to discretionary criteria that may change from round to round – usually the person who organised/founded the Rosca is the one who takes the decision).

Anecdotal evidence points to the presence of at least two types of Roscas (or *Huis*) in Vietnam: commercial (bidding) *Huis* and family-based (random or discrete) Roscas. A professional *Hui* organiser who has the assets and prestige usually founds the *Hui*. The organiser (sometimes in cooperation with the participants) proposes the rules of the *Hui*. This includes the amount of capital (typically in cash) that should be contributed in each round, and the interval between meetings (days, weeks or months). More often than not, the organiser and the participants do not know each other in advance, making the participation in such a *Hui* a bit of a gamble for all parties. No guarantees exist that the founder or individual participant will not run away/fail to make payments. As a consequence, the interest rate levels that can be calculated from the winning bids in each round are found to be quite high – typically

50–300 per cent higher than what can be obtained in commercial banks.

In the family-based *Hui* all participants are, as indicated by its name, acquainted with one another by being relatives or friends. One of them is chosen to be the organiser, but all members typically agree upon the rules and terms. The member who is to receive the pool in a given round is either selected by lot or by common agreement. The order of rotation is typically based on an intra-group comparison of individual member's perceived need for the pool. The organiser is responsible for the implementation of the *Hui* and will typically collect member contributions in each round. For undertaking these duties he or she almost always receives the pool in the first round. This type of *Hui* often has contributions in the form of rice and/or money.

Based on the anecdotal evidence, family *Huis* appear in predominantly rural and traditional settings, while commercial *Huis* appear in more market-based, urban environments. This lends support to the hypotheses originally proposed by Clifford Geertz. According to Geertz (1962), the choice between Roscas reflects a gradual process of modernisation where the eventual dominance of the market-based relationships will lead to the demise of the random and discrete Roscas. This is, however, in contrast with later theories put forward by Ardener (1965) and Besley *et al.* (1993). They propose that the choice between different types of Roscas reflects special characteristics of the group and the environment in which they operate.

Loans from friends and relatives are probably the most important source of credit for households. A loan is typically provided if a household suffers from difficulties due to, for example, disease or floods, or if a household is facing a major event such as a wedding or is building a house. This kind of financial assistance is often given without incurring interest payments. It is, however, not only households that rely on this type of credit. A survey of 407 enterprises in Ha Noi, Hai Phong, Hai Hung, Song Be and Ho Chi Minh City (Hao *et al.* 1996) revealed that 35 per cent of those surveyed borrowed from relatives and friends to establish their enterprise.

Private lending is essentially deference on payments for goods delivered. Suppliers selling on credit are the lenders and the buyers are the borrowers. Lending procedures are simple. Lenders give the goods to the borrowers when they sign in the 'debt' book of lenders. The duration of a loan is typically a production and/or business period, while the interest level typically depends on the price of the goods delivered, ranging from 0 per cent to 5 per cent per month.

The 1993 Vietnamese Living Standards Survey (VLSS) provides some indications of the importance of informal finance. According to the VLSS, 73 per cent of all households used informal credit. It was moreover found that funds from family members, friends and neighbours supplied up to 40 per cent of the credit to private households, moneylenders supplied about 30 per cent, and only about 25 per cent of total household credit originated from formal banks and other sources.

The Vietnam–Sweden Mountain Rural Development Programme (1999) confirms the importance of informal credit, finding that more than 50 per cent of households participating in a survey in the northern mountainous provinces had no access to formal credit and consequently had to rely on informal credit. The major constraints to accessing credit from the formal financial institutions were found to be: lack of assets, lack of land-use-rights required for land to be used as collateral and lack of basic knowledge of how the formal financial system operates.

The importance of informal credit is also confirmed by a 2002 survey of 707 manufacturing SMEs in seven urban and rural provinces in Vietnam. Table 1.5 depicts the sources of credit of 1,072 loans taken by the 707 SMEs. It supports both the claim that friends and relatives are an important source of credit and the claim made by Ninh (2003) that moneylenders do not play a large role as providers of productive credit, focusing instead on distress and consumption credit needs of households.

Just over half (56 per cent) of the 707 SMEs only accessed credit from formal sources, one third (33 per cent) relied only on credit from informal sources, while the remaining 11 per cent relied on both informal and formal sources of credit. This can be interpreted as lending support to the notion that informal credit does not necessarily represent the second-best option. In many cases, the services and products offered by the informal sector are perceived

Table 1.5: Sources of credit in survey of 707 SMEs (2002)

Source of credit	No. of loans	Frequency
Private moneylender	46	4.3 %
Friends and relatives	376	35,1 %
Government banks	326	30,4 %
Private banks	19	1,7 %
Non-state enterprises	69	6,4 %
Other	237	22,1 %
Total	1,072	100 %

Source: Rand *et al.* (2004)

as being superior to those offered by the formal sector. This can be due to lower interest rates (for example credit obtained from family and friends) and/or lower transaction costs (through more rapid dispersion of credit and/or less paperwork).

Dat (1998) cites the results of a study of 150 rural households in the Red River Delta in 1996. Here it was found that total costs of getting a loan of 1 million dong from the formal sector were higher than those associated with a similar loan from the local money-lender – despite the fact that interest rates were lower in the formal sector. This lower price was, however, outweighed by transaction costs associated with getting a formal-sector loan. Very poor people applying for small loans are thus better off relying on the informal financial sector. The informal sector can thus be both complementary or a substitute for the formal sector. Accordingly, the formal sector must take both the presence and the reactions of the informal sector into account when designing and offering financial products and services.

NOTES

1   The description of the Vietnamese political system as being character-ised by a low degree of competitiveness within and between govern-

ment institutions is in line with McCarthy (2001), who argues that consensus governance remains the ruling paradigm in Vietnam.

2 The standard measure is annual deaths per thousand soldiers with each death replaced with a new soldier.

3 The other determinants include: the level of economic development, geographical endowments, religious diversity, ethnic diversity, openness to international trade, number of years the country has been independent since 1776, transplant effect, initial endowments, political environment and the power of the central government over the judiciary branches of the government.

4 Appendix A contains more detailed information about the size and operations of the four large SOCBs.

5 Many of the joint-stock banks established in the first phase were affiliated with SOEs

6 See Gibson and Tsakalotos (1994) for more on this subject.

7 Some of the JSBs established during this period also supplanted former CCs. As a consequence these new JSBs were burdened by bad debts from the onset (Ninh 2003).

8 More formally the prime ministerial decision 390/TTg, dated 27 July 1993, permitted the pilot establishment of the PCF system.

9 The foreign banks are: Bank Dagang Nasional Indonesia, Public Bank Malaysia, Korea First Bank and Daewoo Securities, and the Thai Siam Commercial and Charoen Pokhand Group.

10 The problems encountered by many of the JSBs toward the end of this period are described in Section 1.3 earlier in this chapter.

11 Currently 15 branches of foreign banks are operating in Vietnam, including major international banks such as Deutsche Bank (Germany), Bank of America and CitiBank (USA), Standard Chartered (Great Britain), Credit Lyonnaise (France), ANZ Bank (Australia), State Bank of Krung Thai Bank (Thailand) and National Bank of Kuwait. In addition, there are 62 representative offices from 20 nations operating in Vietnam.

12 The driving factor underlying a practice of holding dollars as a medium of exchange is that the opportunity cost of holding dong instead of dollars may rise significantly during periods of macroeconomic instability and high inflation, leading residents to opt for dollars instead

13 The use of dollars to store value originates from residents' desire to minimise their portfolio risk and variance. This implies that prudent

savers and investors increase dollars holdings if they expect a future increase in inflation.

14 Klump and Gottwald (2003) argue that the Vietnamese government's acceptance of currency substitution was a 'helpful strategy' during the period of disinflation because it helped restore and maintain confidence in the future value of the dong.

15 This corresponds to the amount of real resources appropriated by the government through the printing of money.

16 Historically, the limited success in collecting income taxes in combination with the relatively recent introduction of VAT (in 1999), suggests that seignorage has been a very important source of government revenue in Vietnam. This further acerbates the importance of reducing the level of dollarisation in the economy.

17 According to the balance of payment statistics, net private transfers amounted to US$ 1.1 billion in 2001 and was at this level for the previous three years also (World Bank 2003)

18 The only exception is the South during the war.

19 The recent increase is all the more remarkable in light of the fact that the SBV recently tightened legislation in order to make it less attractive for banks to offer foreign currency deposits.

CHAPTER 2

The East Asian Financial Crisis and its aftermath, 1997–2003

The absence of a liberalised capital account in combination with an inconvertible currency spared the Vietnamese banking system from the detrimental impact of volatile capital flows and institutional distress. In contrast to countries like Indonesia, Korea and Malaysia, the Vietnamese banking sector was to a large extent shielded from the direct effects of the East Asian Financial Crisis.[1]

One of the observed direct effects of the crisis was that enterprises, expecting a devaluation of the VND, chose to hold foreign currency rather than sell it to the banks. This led to an excessive demand for foreign currency on the inter-bank market. As a consequence the inter-bank market for foreign currency almost ceased to exist as the daily volume of transactions dropped from US$ 8 million to below US$ 200,000. This left the SBV with the burden of supplying foreign currency until a decree was passed requiring firms to sell 80 per cent of their foreign exchange to banks (later reduced to 50 per cent). The SBV furthermore decided upon a 10 per cent devaluation of the official exchange rate to the US$ in August 1998, reducing the perceived pressure for devaluation and the demand for foreign currency.

The principal indirect effect of the EAFC on the financial sector was a deterioration of bank assets as bank customers and debtors experienced falling export earnings and/or a reduction in foreign direct investments. As can be seen from Figure 2.1, foreign direct investments (FDI) had, however, already begun to fall in the years leading up to the crisis – possibly reflecting the aforementioned already visible structural problems in the Vietnamese economy. In addition, Vietnamese enterprises and banks had borrowed heavily in foreign currency to take advantage of lower interest rates in a steady exchange rate environment. The devaluation of the dong in August 1998 thus worsened the balance sheets of both banks and bank customers.

The initial government response to the looming crisis was one of denial. Press coverage on the banking system was restricted following the first signs of problems in early 1997 – i.e. before the East Asian Financial Crisis. By classifying information relating to the banking sector as state secrets, the government could furthermore penalise anyone who reported on financial sector problems with up to 15 years in prison.

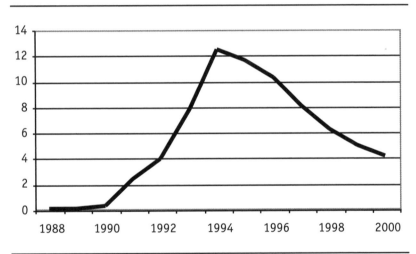

Figure 2.1: Foreign direct investments, net inflows (per cent of GDP)

Source: WDI (2002)

With the onset of the crisis and the resulting unrest in a number of East Asian countries (most notably Indonesia in January 1998), it became clear that the continuation of financial-sector reforms could conflict with the government's overall desire to maintain social and political stability and control. Fear of losing control made the Vietnamese approach towards further reforms even more piecemeal and cautious than it had been earlier. Albeit the need for further comprehensive reforms was stressed in official communiqués from a number of Central Committee plenums, it appears to have been more rhetoric than reality. Consequently, Vietnam did not follow the repeated advice of international agencies (led by the World Bank and IMF) in the years following the EAFC to implement a second round of comprehensive reforms – a 'Doi Moi 2'.

Instead, the initial policy response to the crisis was to use the banking sector to stabilize and support the crisis-stricken SOEs rather than addressing the inherent severe problems in the banking sector. The following are examples of some of the measures introduced in 1998 to help the SOEs through the SOCBs:

- Abolishing the requirement for SOEs to put up collateral when borrowing from SOCBs (essentially permitting SOCBs to lend to loss-making SOEs as long as they had submitted a business plan);

- Offering lower interest rates to SOEs;

- Allowing the rescheduling of loans to troubled SOEs from 1–3-year terms to 1–5-year terms. In addition, some SOEs had their non-performing loans written off.

The combination of the economic crisis, the devaluation and the above mentioned measures represented a heavy financial burden for the SOCBs. The government's response to the possibility of a crisis in the SOCB sector, however, resembled that which introduced support the SOEs a year earlier. In short, the government chose to introduce compensating measures that addressed the symptoms rather than the underlying causes of the crisis. These measures included lowering the income tax rate for the banking system from 45 to 32 per cent (January 1999), lowering the reserve requirement ratio from 8 to 5 per cent (March 1999) and direct allocation of funds (September 1999).[2]

Since data are not available on bank financial performance and the size of their non-performing loans (NPLs) during this period, it is difficult to gauge the severity of the problems and the extent to which the mitigating measures worked. The problems associated with the high ratio of NPLs in the banking sector and the measures subsequently proposed to resolve these problems are discussed in more detail below.[3]

The SOCBs were, however, not the only financial institutions encountering trouble following the crisis. After experiencing a rapid growth in lending over the period prior to the EAFC the JSBs now encountered a multitude of difficulties. As mentioned previously, the majority of the JSBs were established rapidly in the years following the initial liberalisation of the financial sector. This rapid establishment, in concert with the fact that some of them were based on failed CCs and others had close ties to SOEs, can perhaps help explain why they subsequently ran into problems. Other contributing factors were poor risk management and the use of outdated technology.

As a result, more than two-thirds of JSBs failed to meet the minimal requirement for chartered capital in 1998.[4] When the magnitude of the problems in the JSB sector became clear to the government, the SBV was made responsible for undertaking independent diagnostic audits of all the JSBs during 1998–99. On the basis of these audits, the JSBs were subsequently classified into four types and a restructuring strategy for each type was developed. The financial assessments of 48 JSBs were completed by the end of 2000, and based on these the SBV completed and approved restructuring plans for all the 48 JSBs. As a result, 13 JSBs were placed under special supervision/control by the SBV, two had their banking licenses revoked and one was forced to merge. Later in 2001 the license of another JSB was revoked, and the SBV announced that a number of other JSBs would follow unless improvements were recorded in central prudential ratios. In addition, the legislation governing the JSBs was strengthened, requiring them to meet a higher minimum level of capitalisation as well as loan loss provisioning standards.

As for the People's Credit Fund system, its status at the end of 1999 was that a total of 971 Local Credit Funds (LCFs) with a total of 714,000 members had been established in communes and districts. The LCFs were controlled by 21 Regional Credit Funds who all were members of the Central PCF. At this point, the LCFs had mobilised a total of 2,220 billion dong in deposits, of which 157 billion dong was capital put up by founding members while the remainder was mobilised funds. The total value of outstanding loans was 1,816 billion dong of which 4.14 per cent according to Vietnamese accounting standards was classified as overdue debt. The operational performance of the RCFs hence appeared to be satisfactory, meeting the LCF's demand for capital and mobilising about 400 billion dong annually. Chapter 5 will focus on some of the problems facing the PCF system in terms of meeting the demand for financial services in the rural markets.

On the regulatory side, the pre-crisis ordinances and decisions relating to the SBV primarily addressed the separation from the actual financial system and only to a limited extent the separation from the political system. This process was initiated with the Law on the State Bank passed in October 1998. In this respect, the Law on the State Bank represents an important step towards separating the SBV from the political system and establishing it as an autonomous entity on a par with the executive, legislative and judiciary branches of government. The Law on the State Bank made it clear that SBV should perform the functions of state management on monetary issues and banking activities, including:

- Participating in the formulation of the social and economic development strategy and plan of the state;

- Developing national monetary policy to be examined by the government and submitted to the National Assembly for deciding and organising its implementation. This included a development strategy for banking and credit institutions in Vietnam;

- Developing projects of law and ordinance and other monetary and banking operation projects. Promulgate legal documents and regulations;

- Examining and inspecting banking operations, and resolve violations in monetary business and banking operations;

- Representing Vietnam among international credit institutions and banks if mandated by the president and the government of Vietnam;

- Acting as Bank of Credit Institutions and Bank of Monetary Services for the Government.

In addition, the 1998 Law on the State Bank authorised the SBV to perform a number of central bank functions including the printing and issuing of money, refinancing, executing monetary market and open-market functions, controlling international monetary storage, managing foreign exchange and organising the payment system.

Some experts have argued that the level of independence stipulated by the Law on the State Bank was lower than that bestowed upon the SBV prior to the passing of the law.[5] In this context it is, however, important to remember that the Law on the State Bank was passed at a time when governments throughout the region where trying to restrict and hamper financial sector volatility and innovation. This highly sensitive time for financial regulation can perhaps explain why the Law on the State Bank was more restrictive than practice and legislation in place prior to its passing. While adverse circumstances at the time of the passing of the law might explain its restrictiveness, it does not explain why the law was not changed when circumstances improved.

According to Klump and Gottwald (2003), the EAFC also affected other legislative changes connected with the reforms of the financial sector, more specifically the establishment of a Vietnamese stock market.[6] This had been on the government's agenda since 1992, but it was not until 1999 that the State Security Commission (SSC) approved the decisions that were to govern the market. The stock exchange subsequently opened for business in July 2000. As can be expected the stock market started slowly initially only having five companies listed – all former SOEs. This can in part be attributed to the considerable delays in the announced plans to equitise SOEs (see below), and in part to the prudential regulation put in place to govern entry into the market.[7] In addition, the task of training staff as well as addressing the lack of knowledge about both stocks and stock markets among Vietnamese companies and investors alike also contributed to the slow start.

As the supply of shares was very limited,[8] excess demand caused prices to rise during the first half of 2001. This led the SSC to introduce a number of measures designed to curb demand, including a limit on the number of shares owned by a single investor, a stock price fluctuation band of 2 per cent and a price ceiling. Moreover, more companies were introduced to the market, bringing the number of companies traded on the exchange to 23 (as of January 2004). The stock market is, however, still in the early stages of development, being highly volatile and not a major source of funding for companies.

While the EAFC is likely to have caused delays *vis-à-vis* the introduction of the stock market, the development of new financial markets and institutions proceeded in other areas. One example of a new financial institution is the Vietnam Postal Service Savings Company (VPSC) that was established in 1999. Controlled by the Ministry of Finance, the VPSC has the as its main function the provision of savings products to groups that are excluded from accessing the formal financial market (e.g. women or the rural poor). The savings mobilised are subsequently used to finance development projects (see below). Utilising the existing network of post offices as well as workers in the postal service the VPSC network has grown rapidly since implementation totalling 539 branches in 2002. In addition to offering savings products the VPSC offers nationwide money transfers that in time will rely on a network of computer-linked offices.

The World Bank (2002b) has expressed concern over whether the savings mobilisation by the VPSC and the lending on of funds to policy lending is an appropriate mechanism in the long run: first, because the skills necessary to offer financial services might not be available; second, because building a parallel structure outside the formal financial system and existing financial institutions assigned to perform similar tasks might not be efficient; third, because the possibility exists that the VPSC would employ some of the funds raised to subsidise its operations. Finally, there is the issue of using the funds for investment in socially motivated lending, which may not provide a sufficiently high return to cover the costs of raising the deposits.

Another market that was opened in 1999 was the insurance market. Here, the government-owned company Bao Viet had held a monopoly until the market was opened for foreign insurance companies in joint-venture agreements with domestic firms and 100 per cent domestically owned companies in 1993 and 1995, respectively.[9] Until 1999 four new companies were established, but Bao Viet continued to dominate the market. However, in 1999 foreign-owned insurance companies were allowed to obtain a licence and enter the Vietnamese market, albeit only in selected areas such as life insurance. The opening of the insurance market was further accelerated by the US Bilateral Trade Agreement (USBTA) signed in July 2000 (see below). The USBTA stipulated that entry into all types of insurance would be opened for US majority-owned companies and wholly US-owned companies after three and five years, respectively (World Bank 2003).

Although the insurance market is still small in absolute terms, it is nevertheless very interesting to track the development in an area where foreign companies have been allowed to compete on equal terms: namely the market for life insurance (see Table 2.1).

Table 2.1: Market share of life insurance companies (per cent)

	Bao Viet	Bao Minh	Prudential	Manulife	Allianz & AGF	American Int.
2000	76	1	15	7	2	1
2001	54	1.5	29.8	10. 8	2.2	3.8

Source: Thong (2003)

The rapid growth of the market shares, especially Prudential and Manulife, is all the more remarkable given that the size of the entire market for life insurance (as measured by the value-written direct premiums) grew by 115 per cent from 2000 to 2001. One explanation for the rapid growth of foreign companies in both absolute and relative terms is that other available insurance options are viewed as less attractive (hence the growth in absolute terms) and that foreign-owned companies are perceived as more reliable than domestic (hence the growth in relative terms). Finally, part of the rapid growth in foreign companies must be ascribed to their comparative advantage in marketing.

Financial lease companies are another example of an emerging financial market institution in Vietnam. Financial lease companies undertake medium- and long-term credit activities, by leasing machines, equipment, means of transport and others types of capital to manufacturers. In short, the financial lease companies buy machines according to the requirements of the leasing party (e.g. a manufacturer), which subsequently uses and leases according to a specified non-annullable contract. At the termination of the contract, the leasing party can choose between using their option to buy the equipment or to continue hiring according to conditions as specified in a new contract.

The official permission to establish financial leasing was granted in 1995 when the government issued Decree 64, stipulating a statute on the organisation and operation of financial companies. It is, however, still a relatively small market as financial lease companies have only gradually become an accepted alternative by enterprises. Hence, the total capital channelled through FLCs loans only amounted to 1 per cent of total commercial bank credit by the end of 2000, and the SBV has only granted a licence to nine financial lease companies over the period from February 1996 to January 2002. Two of the nine companies are joint-stock companies, two are fully financed by foreign capital and five are owned directly by the SOCBs.

While the financial sector slowly diversified[10] and developed as a result of past and current reforms, economic growth did not pick up in the years following the EAFC. As a consequence in 2000 the government recommended a substantial loosening of overall credit growth in an effort to boost the domestic economy

Despite the very high growth rate of credit in 2000 and a simultaneous recovery in neighbouring East Asian counties,[11] Vietnam did not obtain GDP growth rates comparable to the very high pre-crisis level (see Table 2.2).[12] The three-year slow-down in economic growth following the EAFC, in combination with the government's desire to uphold the performance legitimacy achieved through high growth and prosperity,[13] provides one explanation as to why the government finally decided to increase the pace of financial sector reforms in 2001. Another view is that the government finally yield to pressure for new reforms from the donor community, led by the IMF and World Bank. This view is, however, dismissed by McCarthy

Table 2.2: Overall credit growth and credit growth to the SOEs (per cent)

	1998	1999	2000	2001	2002
Overall credit growth rate	16.4	19.2	38.1	21.4	22.2
Growth rate of credit for the SOEs	22.9	42.5	28.7	14.0	9.0

Note: Credit to SOEs from the banking system is defined as the sum of all claims on the SOEs by the banking system; SOEs are defined as wholly state-owned companies
Sources: Overall credit growth rate: SBV *Annual Report*, 2002;
Growth rate of credit for the SOEs (as of December of the given year): World Bank (2002b)

(2001) who points to the Vietnamese tradition of consensus governance and the large influence of the Communist Party (who like almost any government wants to remain in control) as the key reason for why donors 'cannot make big things happen in Vietnam'.

As mentioned earlier, the transparency surrounding decision-making processes within the ruling elite comes close to opaque closure. One can therefore only guess at the reason for the official return to more comprehensive reforms but, as was the case at the start of the Doi Moi reforms in 1986, a Communist Party Conference again marked the official turning point. This time the Ninth Party Congress held in March 2001 signalled a new commitment towards more comprehensive reforms. In preparation for this congress, the government had undertaken a number of strategic planning exercises including the formulation of a development strategy for the period 2001-10. In addition, ten-year strategies and five-year plans for key sectors had been prepared by the responsible line ministries.

After the congress the government further committed itself to reforms by requesting and obtaining a three-year assistance arrangement from the IMF and the World Bank. This first agreement between Vietnam and the Bretton Woods institutions increased the pressure for early and sustained reforms of both the SOCB and the SOE sectors. The government also approved an overall reform framework for the SOCBs. The reforms focused on restructuring the banks by addressing the problem of non-performing loans through a phased recapitalisation. To avoid problems of moral hazard and increase the competition in the banking sector the recapitalisation was made dependent upon progress in measures aimed at enhancing transparency through, among other things, a gradual implementation of international accounting and auditing standards. In addition, policy lending through the SOCBs was to be phased out and moved to a specialised policy bank (see more below). The government consequently announced that policy-induced lending would be phased out 'except under limited and explicitly identified circumstances with government guarantees'.[14]

The SOCBs had long been characterised by weak balance sheets burdened by a large amount of non-performing loans (NPLs) resulting mainly from failed policy lending to SOEs in the past. The exact magnitude of the NPL problem was (and is still) not known as estimates vary considerably according to the source and the accounting standards used. According to the IMF (2003), the four large SOCBs had accumulated NPLs totalling 23 billion dong. This is equivalent to twice their capital, 5 per cent of GDP and 15 per cent of all outstanding credit. However, according to the official Vietnamese estimates shown in Table 2.3, the size of the NPLs is somewhat lower than estimated by the IMF.

Table 2.3: Non-performing loans (per cent of total outstanding loan volume)

	1996	1997	1998	1999	2000
Entire bank sector	9.3	12.3	13.0	12.5	11.4
State commercial banks only	11.0	11.9	11.2	11.1	10.8
Joint-stock commercial banks only	4.2	13.5	13.9	13.1	12.4

Source: *Assessment of Vietnams Economy's* (1999) CIEM/Vietnam/ Australia and *Annual Report* of the SBV, 2000.

Another estimate by the IMF employing diagnostic audits based on international accounting standards has, however, estimated that non-performing loans in SOCBs constituted up to 30 per cent of outstanding loans over the period 1996–99. In addition, informal assessments suggest that the ratio of NPLs to total loan value was substantially higher than 30 per cent in 2000.[15]

One reason for the huge discrepancy between the official estimate and estimates made by outsiders is the practice of rolling over old loans that is believed to be widespread in the Vietnamese banks and in the SOCBs in particular. Another explanation is that Vietnamese accounting standards (as mentioned previously) dictate that provisioning should be made only for the arrears and not for the total loan in the case of loan default. This practice, despite an instruction to all SOCBs to phase in international accounting standards, has yet to be abolished (IMF 2003). In addition, the situation was made even more difficult by SOCBs not having to base provisioning on overdue debt or to adjust it according to risk levels. Instead, commercial banks were required to use 10 per cent of profits after taxes for risk provisions, an amount that is clearly insufficient for the purpose.

Decision 488 of November 2000 started the process of gradually changing Vietnamese accounting standards by requiring that risk provisioning should based on overdue debt and that commercial bank assets should be classified into four groups depending on their assessed risk. The regulation concerning provisioning was subsequently further strengthened by Decision 1627 of December 2001 stipulating that the entire loan balance should be classified as overdue if interest and/or principal payments were overdue. In addition, it was made clear that provisioning should be based on the estimated risk level when the loan was disbursed rather than after the loan became overdue. Finally, Decision 1627 stipulated that risk provisioning funds could be used only to cover losses for which objective reasons (such as natural disasters) could be identified. While the passing of the necessary legislation clearly represents initial progress, the actual implementation of the changes has proven to be very difficult. The IMF (2003) consequently describes the implementations of the new loan classification rules as 'non-transparent'.

This lack of transparency was a key factor behind the decision to let each SOCB undergo independent audits based on international accounting standards. These audits are not made available to the public but have been occurring annually[16] and have resulted in key measures that each bank has to carry out. In addition to the audits, it was decided that credit exposure on a single loan project was not allowed to the more than 15 per cent of a bank's chartered capital; special monitoring of bank credit to 200 SOEs with large debts was also put in place.

Resolving the NPL problem was (and is), however, crucially dependent upon the financial discipline and operational performance of the creditors – the SOEs. Here, a five-year SOE equitisation plan with annual targets specified for the first three years was presented in 2001. The plan involved around 2,000 of a total of 5,500 SOE since the government chose to maintain ownership in 'strategic' (mainly infrastructure) sectors. The plan also included steps to strengthen SOE financial discipline and the introduction of safety nets for resulting redundant labour. Looking at Table 2.4, however, it becomes clear that even from the outset the plan fell far behind targets.

Table 2.4: SOE equitisation targets and transformations to date

	2001 Target	2002 Actual	2003 Target
Total	710	282	651
Equitisation	478	204	460
Transfer, sale	55	57	49
Liquidation	90	21	68
Other	87	0	74

Note: Actual performance in 2003 only covers the period up to May.
Source: IMF (2003)

In addition, the SOEs scheduled for equitisation are generally small, accounting for a total of 24 per cent of SOE employment and a mere 3 per cent of total SOE debt. The plan for the rest of the (larger and more heavily indebted) SOEs is to increase their autonomy and accountability in an attempt to improve their incentives to perform. As this would take a long time in almost any economy, the general conditions of limited SOE transparency and low profitability are unlikely to change in the near future.

One implication of the slow SOE reforms is that improvements in the operating conditions of the SOCBs becomes highly dependent on the government keeping it's promise to shift policy lending to policy-lending banks. Decision number 131 of October 2002 outlined the creation of the policy-lending bank the Bank for Social Policies (BSP). The BSP came into operation in early 2003. It is based on the already established Bank for the Poor (see Chapter 5). In addition, funds for the BSP were transferred from various government-controlled social funds including the Job Creation Fund and the Fund for Poor and Hardworking Students. Early in 2003 the BSP received a transfer of funds amounting to 5 billion dong from the government budget. The bank has its own administrative staff, but (as was the case of the Bank for the Poor) relies on the branch offices and staff of the VBARD for actual lending operations.

In addition, the government had already (as mentioned previously) transferred some of the policy lending to the Development Assistance Fund (DAF). DAF lending is funded by the Ministry of Finance (MOF) onlending deposits raised by the Vietnam Postal Service Savings Company (VPSC). According to the World Bank (2002b) it is, however, unclear whether the interest payments made by DAF to the MOF are sufficient to cover costs of raising the deposits through VPSC. If not, this constitutes an implicit government subsidy to the DAF as well as an implicit government guarantee to VPSC that their costs for providing financial services will be covered.

Looking again at Table 2.2 one can, however, not fail to notice that 2000 was the first year where credit growth to the SOE sector was lower than overall credit growth. Whether this is because BSP and DAF had taken over some of the policy induced lending or because the SOCBs responded to increasing credit demand in the private sector is not clear. It is, however, clear that the SOCBs are continuing to undertake policy lending. The World Bank (2002b) describes examples of large dollar loans to infrastructure projects. In order to circumvent the 15 per cent maximum exposure on a single project, the SOCBs have formed syndicates offering the loans at what appear to be very favourable conditions. In addition, SOCBs are reported to continue to lend to troubled SOEs in, for example, the sugar industry.

While refraining from giving direct orders to the SOCBs, the government pressure on bank management has been applied through government 'advice' to provide the loans. Hence, the government has clearly not abided by the initial decision to restrict loan-reduction and/or write-offs to SOEs that are subject to liquidation, divestiture or equitisation under the SOE reform programme. In this context it is, however, interesting and encouraging to note that for the first time one SOCB in December 2003 declined to follow the government's 'advice' to give loans to a SOE applicant – signalling (perhaps) more SOCB autonomy.

Despite the fact that SOCBs have failed to implement the recommendations following the diagnostic audits (IMF 2003) and that policy lending is continuing (albeit to a lesser degree), the government went ahead and approved the start of SOCB recapitalisation in December 2002. As can be seen from Table 2.5, a second release of recapitalisation funds followed in 2003.

Table 2.5: Recapitalisation of SOCBs (in billions of Vietnamese dong)

Bank	Charter capital 2001	First stage of recapitalisation Dec 2002	Second stage of recapitalisation 2003	Charter capital Sep 2003
VBARD	2,279	1,500	700	4,471
VBID	1,000	1,200	1,450	3,650
Vietcombank	1,100	1,000	400	2,500
Incombank	1,045	1,000	-	2,245

Source: Trong (2003)

Notwithstanding the recapitalisation, the SOCBs still have trouble meeting the specified capital adequacy ratio[17] (CAR) of 8 per cent currently having a CAR around 3–5 per cent. As a consequence, discussions are pending to identify alternative ways of raising

funds for SOCB recapitalisation. A model currently under consideration is to allow the SOCBs to issue bonds that upon later stage
equitisation can be converted into equity.[18]

The medium-term consequences of the decision to initiate recapitalisation are, however, far more serious than any failure to
meet the required CAR. By deciding to begin recapitalisation without the SOCBs having met the stipulated requirements, the government
undermines SOCB incentives to reform, essentially signalling that
recapitalisation will take place regardless of reform performance.
The IMF (2003) and the World Bank (2002b) are rightly concerned.
It appears that SOCB reforms are slipping.

The total costs of the banking reform and recapitalisation are
still uncertain. The preliminary estimate (IMF 2001) set the total
capital costs at 17 trillion dong – amounting to approximately 4
per cent of GDP in 2001. More recent estimates based on the
diagnostic audits and the expectation that a part of the massive
growth in new loans since the beginning of the SOCB reforms will
also turn out to be non-performing (without adequate provisioning
made at the time of making the loan) lead to a higher estimate of
around 7 per cent of GDP in 2003 (IMF 2003). The government has
announced that the cost of the banking reform and recapitalisation will be treated as an extraordinary outlay. It will be financed
through internal bank resources, including loan recoveries and
strengthened profitability, non-negotiable government bonds, bank
bonds, external support and government budgetary resources.

As for the NPL problem, the rapid growth in credit depicted in
Table 2.2 in combination with the fact that SOCBs appear to have
been more focused increasing the volume of their lending rather
than increasing its profitability, imply that the total amount of
loans has increased while the inflow of new NPLs is likely to have
been negligible. As the NPL ratio is measured as a per cent of total
loans, an increase in the denominator is likely to be partly responsible
for the drop in NPL ratio observed in Table 2.6.

The fact that the SOCBs as part of their rapid increase in lending have expanded to segments and sectors outside their respective
areas of expertise, in concert with the limited progress in improving
the financial skills and risk management of the SOCBs, indicates

Table 2.6: Ratio of non-performing loans to total loans (per cent)

	1998	1999	2000	2001	2002
NPL ratio	13.0	12.5	11.4	8.5	7.1

Source: CIEM (1999) and SBV *Annual Report* 2002, based on Vietnamese accounting standards).

that matters could deteriorate rapidly if and when the economic growth rate drops. Some progress has, however, also been recorded in the efforts to resolve the NPLs. This will be discussed in detail in Chapter 4. On the other hand, a number of recent initiatives hold a more positive outlook for financial sector development.[19] More specifically, the government established a Registry Centre for Secured Transactions in 2002. The objective of the centre is to resolve conflicting creditor claims on moveable assets (except ships and planes). In addition, the government also set up a Credit Information Centre tasked with providing information about borrowers to banks. When operational, the two centres could improve overall transparency and attractiveness of the market for private credit. It will, for example, become more difficult for borrowers to use the same asset for collateral in different banks.

Another positive development is the 2000 implementation of a deposit insurance scheme. The massive loss of savings resulting from the collapse of the credit cooperative system and subsequently the problems encountered by the JSBs suggest that this initiative, once it has proved its worth and has become publicly known, is likely to improve the general level of trust in the financial sector. The process of establishing a deposit insurance scheme has been long under way, beginning with the first legislation passed in 1997. The Deposit Insurance Agency (DIA) was established as a separate legal entity but works closely with the SBV. The insurance offered by the DIA is provided to all residents in Vietnam and covers up to a maximum of 30 million dong. One exception is that deposits in foreign currency that are not covered by the scheme. Given that foreign currency-denominated deposits amount to almost half[20] of total deposits, the soundness of this decision should be considered as should the potential implications for financial sector stability in the event of a crisis. Deposits made by enterprises are another exception from the current deposit insurance scheme, but the often close links between an SME and a household suggests that the World Bank (2002b) recommendation that omission be rectified also ought to be reconsidered.

In addition to these positive developments on the institutional side, the government has also latterly allowed further liberalisation of interest rates. The process of deregulating interest rates began in 1996 when banks were allowed to set interest rates on dong deposits, and liberalisation of interest rates on deposits in foreign currency followed in 1999. In August 2000 a new base rate mechanism was introduced. This entailed widening the allowable range in which banks set lending rates, coupled with a further relaxation of controls. In November 2001 the interest rate ceilings on foreign currency loans were abolished. The banks based in Vietnam were, however, not allowed to set interest rates on foreign currency loans at their own discretion: they were required to consult with the SBV, taking international market rates and the domestic supply and demand in account. Finally, in 2002 lending rates in domestic currency were liberalised. This step has, however, not materialised into significant changes in actual dong lending rates that more or less remain at the level prior to deregulation. The World Bank (2003) points to lack of competition between banks, rapid growth in monetisation and interference by the SBV as possible explanations for the lack of fluctuation.

Another market undergoing a gradual deregulation is the market for foreign exchange. Until 1990 the government exercised complete control over this market through a fixed-exchange regime. As foreign trade with the former Soviet bloc was conducted on a convertible rouble basis, foreign exchange management was limited to setting the official rates. Over the period 1990–2001 the government gradually loosened the fixed exchange rate seeking, instead to control the dollar/dong exchange rate through change in the official exchange rates and/or the width of the trading band. In February 1999 the SBV abolished the official rate, opting instead for a crawling-peg to the US$. In practice, this suggests that the

Table 2.7: Dong depreciation to the dollar, 1992–2001 (per cent)

	1992	'93	'94	'95	'96	'97	'98	'99	2000	2001
Dong depreciation	-8.1	2.6	1.9	-0.3	0.3	11.6	12.7	0.9	3.5	3.9

Source: State Bank of Vietnam. The end of the year exchange rate is used to calculate the dong depreciation.

exchange rate to the dollar is set daily by the SBV and then allowed to fluctuate according to supply and demand within a 0.1 per cent band. However, as the SBV remains the most powerful participant in the market, it is still able to control interest rate movements within this band.

Table 2.8: USBTA commitments in the banking sector

Date implemented	Action stipulated by the USBTA
December 2001	No. of US branch banks no longer subject to a country quota National treatment for US shares in JSBs
Phased in from 2001–10	Joint ventures with US equity between 30 and 49% are allowed
December 2002	US branch banks allowed to accept dong deposits up to 50% of legal paid in capital
December 2004	US branch banks accorded full national treatment US branch banks allowed to take initial mortgage interest in Land-Use Rights (LURs) held by foreign invested enterprises US branch banks are allowed to acquire and use mortgages of LURs for liquidation in the case of default US branch banks have access to rediscounting, swap and forward facilities of the SBV
December 2010	100% US subsidiary banks allowed

Source: Riedel (2004)

As can be seen in Table 2.7, the practice of having the SBV set the daily exchange rate has resulted in a gradual depreciation in relation to the dollar. In the medium to long run the latest most important events could, however, turn out to be the signing of the Bilateral Trade Agreement with the US (USBTA) in July 2000 and the negotiations about Vietnamese membership of the WTO that began in 2002. As already mentioned in the discussion about the Vietnamese insurance market, the USBTA requires Vietnam to gradually open its market to US companies. The consequences of the USBTA for the banking sector are outlined in Table 2.8. If Vietnam over the same period joins the WTO, the WTO ban on preferential treatment of individual countries will ensure that similar rights are accorded to all foreign companies. These developments in the insurance market indicate that allowing foreign banks to compete on equal terms with domestic institutions could have ramifications for the both the financial institutions and the regulation and supervision of the sector. The effects of foreign bank entry are discussed in Chapter 3.

CONCLUDING REMARKS

The descriptive analysis presented in this and the previous chapter makes it evident that Vietnam has come a long way in changing its financial market from a centrally coordinated sector to a market economy. New markets and new institutions have been established and new legislation is in place. The gradual approach to reforms has abolished the more direct government control of the financial sector and reduced the still persistent indirect control. As a result, total credit intermediation by the banking sector now amounts to more than 40 per cent of GDP, considerably higher than in many other transitional economies.

The reform process has been gradual and has from time to time been set on the backburner for a period. This is not unusual. Evidence from other countries undergoing similar transitions testifies that financial liberalisation and deregulation is a lengthy and difficult process, occasionally involving setbacks and lack of real progress. A number of factors suggest that the reform process is likely to be even more prolonged in the case of Vietnam. First, the French civil law tradition might slow reforms down. Second, and perhaps more important, the Vietnamese tradition of consensus governance, in concert with the ruling elite's preference for social and political stability, is also likely to act as a brake on reforms. Third, the extensive links between the state-owned productive sector and the financial sector may also cause reforms in Vietnam to last longer. Finally, the early crises in the process of liberalising the sector (most notably the collapse of the system of credit cooperatives) may also restrict the pace of reforms. The reason is that it may take a long time to rebuild trust in the formal financial market which in turn could cause newly established markets to take longer to develop.

The fact that Vietnam was spared from the direct consequences of the East Asian Financial Crisis implied that the Vietnamese response to the crisis would differ considerably from that of the other East Asian countries. While the latter strengthened and broadened reform efforts in response to the crisis, Vietnam imposed a temporary halt to comprehensive reforms – most likely to minimise the risk of social and political instability.

Although Vietnam has come a long way, considerable obstacles to financial sector liberalisation and deregulation remain. The persistence of policy-based lending is one, while the lack of transparency and accountability is another. As for the problem of non-performing loans in the banking sector, it is important to keep in mind that this problem in both the corporate and financial sectors also persists in most of the other East Asian countries that were affected by the EAFC. These countries have also embarked on a process of institutional reform, new banking and accounting standards, disclosure requirements and rules for corporate governance, but, as in Vietnam, the new rules and legislation that have been passed are not rigorously enforced.

Again, a number of factors combine to make it likely that the Vietnamese problems relating to non-performing loans most likely will take even longer to resolve than in neighbouring countries. The first factor is the lack of transparency, as testified by the continued lack of international accounting estimates of the size of the NPL problem. The second factor that is likely to make resolving

NPLs in Vietnam a case apart is the culture of consensus governance blocking most attempts to reform the debt-ridden SOEs. A third factor is that both the banks holding the NPLs and the companies to whom these loans were given are owned and controlled by the government, making it easier for the government to conceal the problem and/or to propose cosmetic solutions to it.

Although reforms (with the possible exception of the period immediately after the EAFC) have proceeded in small steps over the entire period, the growing integration between the Vietnamese economy and the global markets (through the USBTA and a possible WTO membership) could increase pressure on the government to strengthen the regulation and supervision of the Vietnamese financial sector. The regulation and supervision of the Vietnamese banking sector is the topic of the following two chapters, starting with a regional comparison and then subsequently moving on to take a closer look at the SBV.

NOTES

1   The East Asian countries directly affected by the crisis experienced large drops in GDP growth rates. In 1998 the growth rate plunged from a regional pre-crisis average of 7.0 per cent to -13.2 in Indonesia, -10.4 in Thailand, -7.5 in Malaysia, -6.7 in Korea, and -0.6 in the Philippines (Park and Lee, 2002).

2   According to Klump and Gottwald (2003) the government spent US$ 300 million during 1998 and 1999 in an attempt to bolster the chartered capital of the SOCBs.

3   In addition, Chapter 4 contains an analysis of the institutional framework set up by the SBV to resolve the NPL problem.

4   At that time urban JSBs were required to have at least 65 billion dong, while the requirement imposed on rural JSBs was only 2 billion dong (Ninh 2003).

5   See Chapter 4 for an analysis of the current level of state bank independence.

6   The inter-bank market and the market for government bonds are discussed in relation to the SBV in Chapter 4.

7   In order to obtain a licence, a company must list equity of at least 10 billion dong and have recorded a profit for the previous two years

8   According to Ninh (2003) 60–70 per cent of the shares of the initial five companies listed were not traded.

9   This is not a typo. Foreign companies in joint-venture agreements with domestic companies were in fact allowed to enter the market two years prior to fully domestically owned companies. Whether this decision reflects a perception that domestic knowledge about the insurance business was too limited in 1993 is not known.

10   In parallel with the rapid increase in the different types of institutions, the services provided by the formal financial institutions has also increased to include investment brokerage, stock brokerage, issuance of credit cards, financial consultancy services, asset insurance and liability insurance.

11   Park and Lee (2002) find that both the contraction after the EAFC and the following recovery has been more rapid and far greater in East Asia than what could have been predicted from cross-country evidence.

12   According to the World Bank (2002b), GDP growth rose from 4.8 per cent in 1999 to 6.8 per cent in 2000 (preliminary estimate).

13   As pointed out by McCarthy (2001), the Vietnamese government strives to be perceived as caring for people, fighting corruption and ensuring economic development through the gradual loosening of central coordination and planning. In addition, McCarthy points to the legacy of the protracted war against the French and the Americans as a factor that also continues to strengthen the legitimacy of the government.

14   See, Socialist Republic of Vietnam (2001a). It remains to be seen how the government defines 'limited' circumstances.

15   According to Cohen (2003) Standards & Poors estimated that more than 50 per cent of total loan volume would have to be written-off or restructured at concessional rates.

16   Audits for 2000 and 2001 already exist, while 2002 are under way.

17   This is defined as the ratio of equity to total assets.

18   Questions related to both government and corporate bonds in Vietnam are discussed in Chapter 4.

19   The descriptions of the Centre for Secured Transactions, the Credit Information Centre and the Deposit Insurance Agency are based upon information in World Bank (2002b).

20   The World Bank (2002b) sets the share of foreign currency deposits at 45 per cent of total deposits.

CHAPTER 3

A *regional comparison of bank supervision and regulation*

Over the past decade a positive view of financial liberalisation and deregulation has been dampened by the severe repercussions of financial instability and crises. It is increasingly recognised that government failure does not imply market success and that this is especially true in the case of the financial sector. One reason is that problems of moral hazard and adverse selection are of particular concern in the financial sector since most transactions are forward looking and based on mutual trust in the other party's ability to honour contracts. Hence, even if the question of whether financial sector development leads or follows economic growth is still debated, most economists will agree that government interventions to minimise the risk of financial crises are necessary. But in what form and to what degree? Should the government aim at achieving a certain level of financial depth or at the implementation of a certain structure? Or should the government focus more on the establishment of an optimal framework to guide the financial sector, letting market participants choose the direction and speed of change?

The dual role of preventing crises and facilitating the development of the financial sector more or less represents the current consensus view of the role of the government *vis-à-vis* the financial sector.[1] The implication is that policymakers should concentrate on strengthening the legal and regulatory framework rather than to press for a particular financial structure. As a consequence, governments should focus on designing and implementing an effective legal and regulatory environment that supports the evolution of the financial structure. Hence, earlier attempts to control allocation and prices in the financial sector are being replaced by a more passive government, designing the framework and overall conditions suitable for financial growth.

Accepting this view on the role of the government as a starting point, it becomes very interesting to compare Vietnam's financial sector regulation with that of other East Asian economies – in part because the regional comparison presented here could assist an analysis of whether and from whom Vietnam could learn to create a regulatory and legal framework that is more conducive to financial sector development and the prevention of financial crises.

The analysis is presented in five separate sections. The first section compares the level of financial sector competition to that of other countries in the region. This is motivated by the implicit assumption that a highly competitive financial sector is likely to require a different kind of supervision than a non-competitive sector. Hence, a comparison of the level of competitiveness is a necessary prerequisite to the subsequent analysis of regulatory regimes. The next section compares the regulatory framework in Vietnam to that of other countries in the region, followed by a section that compares the set of rules governing banking activities in Vietnam with those of the region. Safety nets, capital adequacy and deposit insurances are next considered, while the chapter ends with an interim conclusion.

LIBERALISATION, PRIVATISATION AND FOREIGN BANK ENTRY

Over the last decade the perception of the potential benefits arising from liberalising financial markets has become more diverse. Some view liberalisation as having universally beneficial effects upon financial sector efficiency. The increased competition that is perceived to follow from liberalisation is thus perceived to have beneficial effects on the size of the consumer surplus and on the overall soundness of the financial system.

One can also find economists who, although they recognise the potential benefits of liberalisation also warn that liberalisation could cause financial sectors to become more fragile and prone to crises. This is argued to be a real risk in countries where the rule of law is weak, corruption is widespread, the bureaucracy inefficient and contract enforcement is ineffective. One of the potentially destabilising effects identified by this latter group is the notion that intense competition between banks can undermine the franchise value of individual branch offices or even entire banks. The erosion of franchise values can subsequently distort risk-taking incentives, leading banks to undertake risky investments in an attempt to gamble for resurrection. This could subsequently destabilise the entire sector, leading the way to financial crises. In an empirical analysis based on data covering 80 countries, Demirgüc-Kunt and Detragiache (1998) find that the available evidence is broadly consistent with the claim the liberalisation increases bank fragility through a negative impact on bank franchise values. Lack of data, however, prevents Demirgüc-Kunt and Detragiache from pursuing the related question of whether increased bank fragility leads to a higher risk of financial crises.

One consequence of the above dissenting views is an increase in policy ambiguity. Should policymakers abandon liberalisation and return to a regime of direct intervention? Can competition turn 'unhealthy' if competition becomes too intense? The answer to the latter question depends on whether the expected benefits from liberalisation are higher than the expected costs from increased financial sector fragility. This is, of course, the easy first answer, but should nevertheless be kept in mind when discussing both the potential benefits of liberalisation and the increased risk of financial crises. As a consequence, policy analysts should carefully consider both short-term and long-term effects of financial sector liberalisation rather than rely on generalisations and a dogmatic approach.

The preceding two chapters made it clear that financial liberalisation in Vietnam still has a long way to go. The activities of the SOCBs continue to be shaped by the specialisation stipulated by past policies and subject to government interference.[2] In addition, the liberalisation of interest rates has yet to result in significant changes in the rates offered, and foreign banks are still not at par with domestic ones.

It is also clear that the Vietnamese financial sector liberalisation has produced results. New markets have emerged and SOCBs are beginning to take advantage of their increased autonomy. The latter caused the World Bank (2002b) to worry that the 'SOCBs may – through uniform strategic choices – end up weakening one another through intense competition if all four become universal banks instead of focusing their efforts on key segments in which they appear to already have competitive advantages'. The World Bank (2002b) subsequently goes on to recommend that 'while not advisable for the government to return to directing the banks in their lending practice, the banks can be indirectly encouraged through a right incentive structure and proper corporate governance to provide services in segments of the economy in which they have a competitive advantage until they are fully commercialized'.

Policy advice of this nature only makes it more interesting to compare the degree of competition in the Vietnamese financial sector with that of other countries in the region. This in turn raises another interesting question: namely, how can one go about measuring the degree of financial sector competition? One approach is to look at the number of agents in the market and the degree of market concentration. The implicit assumption is that a higher number of firms and a lower degree of concentration results in a more competitive market. Another approach is to look at the fraction of bank deposits held by foreign-owned banks. This latter approach assumes that foreign banks are less susceptible to influence from the domestic government, are more efficient and more focused on maximising profits.

Tables 3.1 and 3.2 list the above mentioned indicators for Vietnam and other ASEAN countries. Contrary to what may be believed, bank concentration in Vietnam as measured as the fraction of deposits held by the five largest banks is not higher than in, for example, Thailand. Furthermore, Table 3.2 indicates that the banking sector in Vietnam is less concentrated than that of the average developing country.

One aspect that stands out in both tables is the degree of government ownership in the Vietnamese banking sector. This is very high compared to both the other countries in the region and to the average level in developing countries. This factor should be viewed in the context of the evidence from cross-country analyses

Table 3.1: Financial sector concentration in East Asia (per cent)

	Bank concentration (share of deposits held by the five largest banks)	Share of deposits of the five largest banks held by foreign owned banks	Share of the deposits of the five largest banks held by gov't-owned banks
Vietnam	65	0	80
Cambodia	67	71	16
China	75	n.a.	n.a.
Indonesia	53	7	44
Korea	48	0	30
Malaysia	30	18	0
Philippines	46	13	12
Thailand	75	7	31

Sources: Calculated using information in Barth *et al.* (2001a, 2001b), and information from the World Bank office in Hanoi.
Note: '0' indicates that none of the foreign banks are among the five largest in Vietnam – see Chapter 4 for an estimate of the share of total deposits held by foreign banks.

(Laporta *et al.* 2002, and Barth *et al.* 2001a) indicating that a higher degree of state ownership tends to be associated with lower bank efficiency, less saving and borrowing, lower productivity and slower growth. Furthermore, there is no evidence that government ownership lowers the probability of a banking crisis. Generally the negative effects of state ownership appear to be more severe in developing than in industrialised countries.

Analysing bank performance in 107 countries, Barth *et al.* (2001a) find that tighter entry restrictions tend to increase overhead costs. Barth *et al.* are, however, not able to find a link between bank performance and the actual level of bank concentration. They also find that the likelihood of a major banking crisis is positively associated with greater limitations on foreign bank participation.

Table 3.2: Financial sector concentration in a global perspective (per cent)

	Bank concentration (share of deposits held by five largest banks)	Share of deposits of the five largest banks, which is held by foreign owned banks	Share of the deposits of the five largest banks, which is held by government owned banks
Vietnam	65	0	80
Developed countries	61	25	36
Developing countries	71	10	22

Source: Calculated by using information in Barth, Caprio and Levine (2001a, 2001b), and information from the World Bank office in Hanoi.

Claessens *et al.* (2001) find that the presence of foreign banks improves sector efficiency by creating competitive pressures that stimulate innovations and improve financial services. The nature and degree of these efficiency improvements will, however, depend on the market that is entered and on the type of entrant.

As pointed out by Riedel (2004), the signing of the USBTA and the associated future opening to foreign banks has been the subject of much concern in Vietnam. What will be the implication of levelling the playing field for foreign banks? Will the foreign banks skim the cream and pick up profitable and well-managed Vietnamese firms, leaving the domestic banks with an implicit obligation to serve unprofitable SOEs? Alternatively, one could also imagine a scenario where the entry of foreign banks (as suggested by Barth et al.) result in increased stability, higher efficiency of domestic banks through the increased competition and learning-by-observing effects, and cheaper and more diversified financial services being on offer. Reviewing both cross-country empirical analyses and country case studies, Riedel (2004) finds that: (i) the entry of foreign banks intensifies competition, forcing domestic banks to become more efficient; (ii) that the presence of foreign banks has a tendency to make the domestic markets more stable; and (iii) that foreign banks are liable to focus on their comparative advantages (trade finance and derivatives) and some (mainly manufacturing) sectors of the economy, leaving retail banking, consumer credit and lending to SMEs and to the domestic banks.

The benefits of the entry of foreign banks are of course not universal. Examples of foreign banks overwhelming domestic regulators and exploiting loopholes in weak domestic legislation do exist, as do examples of domestic banks going out of business following the entry of foreign banks.[3] Consequently, domestic legislation and regulation need to be up to the task of increased foreign participation in the sector. Whether or not the future entry of foreign banks into Vietnam is going to benefit domestic banks is uncertain but is likely to depend crucially on the efforts to strengthen the autonomy and accountability of both domestic banks and their supervision and regulation.

If the presence of foreign banks facilitates short-term portfolio investments, their entry may increase the fragility of the domestic financial system. According to Park and Lee (2002), the East Asian Financial Crisis was worsened by the rapid outflow of short-term capital, influenced by herd behaviour and panic among international investors. Given that the Vietnamese capital account is likely to remain closed in the foreseeable future, this is not a relevant risk at present (although it will of course influence when and how the government can open the capital account).

Returning to the regional comparison of the level of competition in the financial sector, it is obvious that bank concentration, although often used, in some cases might be a poor indicator. A high level of concentration does not need to reduce competition, as concentrated systems can be competitive if they are contestable. The rationale is that the potential threat of entry forces market participants to keep rents low in order to dissuade potential competitors from entering the market. For this reason, one should complement the concentration measures cited above with measures of entry and exit restrictions. The idea is that tight restrictions on entry into the banking sector can create monopolies/duopolies that are associated with high interest rate margins and high overhead expenditures.

Table 3.3 depicts some competition regulatory variables for Vietnam and the East Asian region. The data for Vietnam are unfortunately incomplete as it was not possible to obtain information about both the number of applications and the number of rejections hereof. The table does, however, also show the results of a survey of whether or not special legal permissions are required to obtain a licence to operate a bank in the respective countries. Results of this survey are reported as an index ranging from 0 to 8.[4] Higher values indicate a more restrictive system, implying that one would expect that entry into the banking sector was more restricted and/ or deterred. This is in part because there are more grounds for rejecting a licence request and in part because potential applicants know this and therefore refrain from applying.

Looking at Table 3.3, it should be noted that limitations to foreign bank entry exist throughout the region; a significant proportion of both foreign and domestic applications are rejected – the only exceptions are China and to some degree the Philippines. That several countries report that there have been no applications could be due to potential applicants perceiving the sector to be unprofitable or to futile. If the former, potential applicants perceive the respective banking sectors to be so competitive that obtainable rents are too low to justify entry or that they foresee that they will be discriminated against by the domestic regulator.

A glance at the index on the requirements for entry into the banking sector shows that Vietnam has very restrictive entry conditions. One can, however, see that Vietnam does not differ greatly in this respect from the rest of the region. Both Thailand and Cambodia are also found to have highly restrictive entry requirements. The index does suggest that there is still much to be done before the Vietnamese banking environment can be characterised as contestable, or even partly contestable for that matter.

Turning to Table 3.4, it can be seen that entry into banking is not generally more restricted in developing countries than in developed countries. It appears, however, that the fraction of entry denials is significantly higher in developing countries than in developed

Table 3.3: Bank entry regulation in East Asia

	Entry into banking requirement (0–8)	Share of entry applications denied (per cent)	Share of domestic applications denied (per cent)	Share of foreign applications denied (per cent)
Vietnam	8	n.a.[*]	n.a.	n.a.
Cambodia	8	67	70	67
China	6	25	25	No applications
Indonesia	7	60	No applications	60
Korea	7	No applications	No applications	No applications
Malaysia	7	No applications	No applications	No applications
The Philippines	7	34	0	43
Thailand	8	100	100	No applications

Sources: Calculated using information in Barth *et al.* (2001a, 2001b) and information from the World Bank office in Hanoi.
Note: Despite repeated attempts, we have unfortunately not been able to acquire information on the composition and fate of financial sector entry applications in Vietnam.

countries. The difference can perhaps be explained by the higher divergence between *de jure* and *de facto* regulation in developing countries, a lower average quality of banking sector applicants in developing countries or a combination of both.

In conclusion, the available empirical evidence and the legislative framework reviewed in the previous two chapters indicate that the Vietnamese banking sector is characterised by a very low degree of

Table 3.4: Bank entry regulation in a global perspective

	Entry into banking requirement (0–8)	Share of entry applications denied (per cent)	Share of domestic applications denied (per cent)	Share of foreign applications denied (per cent)
Vietnam	8	n.a.	n.a.	n.a.
Developed countries	7.19	3	3	2
Developing countries	7.38	31	28	29

Sources: Calculated using information in Barth *et al.* (2001a, 2001b) and information from the World Bank office in Hanoi.

competition. The lack of interest rate diversification and changes following the deregulation of interest rates bear further testimony to this conclusion by suggesting that informal agreements and/or government pressure further dampen competitive pressures.

BANK SUPERVISION AND REGULATION

Any cross-country comparison of legislation must face the inevitable question: but do those laws actually correspond with actual practice? In the case of Vietnam the descriptive analysis presented in the previous two chapters clearly shows that the answer most likely is 'no'. This is demonstrated by, for example, the official commitment to move policy lending away from the SOCBs versus the fact that the Vietnamese government continues to circumvent its own legislation by giving 'advice' and/or apply pressure on financial sector institutions. This practice is not unique to Vietnam, but the lack of transparency that (naturally) surrounds government interference in any country makes it difficult to say with any certainty whether or not such interference is more widespread/severe in Vietnam. Consequently, one can interpret the comparison of *de jure* practice as an (acknowledged incomplete) proxy for *de facto* practice.

In addition, even if not respected by the government, existing legislation will still serve as a marker for acceptable government behaviour, making it possible for outsiders to criticise the government. It can also be interpreted as a reflection of the government's perception of how the sector is going to be regulated in the distant or not so distant future (once the problems of present undue interference have been solved). Both interpretations add to the potential value of a cross-country comparison of the legislation governing financial sector supervision and regulation.

In order to be able to compare the financial sector legislation across countries we rely on the indicators developed by Barth *et al.* (2001a). By categorising existing legislation and rules according to whether specific measures are judged to be in place Barth *et al.* are able to develop a number of indexes of official supervisory power. This methodology has subsequently been used to create indexes reflecting the strength of the Vietnamese legislation as of December 2002. The timing of the creation is, of course, important as the legislation is constantly changing over time. The index values presented in the tables below do consequently not reflect upon any changes in the legislation between December 2002 and January 2004.

Tables 3.5 and 3.6 list a number of a number of variables intended to capture the degree to which supervisory authorities in Vietnam and other East Asian countries are capable of designing and implementing interventions with the objective of promoting a well-functioning banking industry. More specifically, the number of supervisors per bank is thought to give an indication of the resources available to the regulator. The official supervisory power index looks at existing legislation to see whether the supervisory authorities have the authority to take specific actions to prevent and correct problems. The index rates between 0 and 14, with higher values indicating greater power.

The prompt corrective power index rates between 0 and 6, with higher values indicating the regulator is enforced to act promptly once irregularities are detected. These include whether or not the law establishes predetermined levels of bank solvency deterioration that force automatic actions, such as intervention. The restructuring power and the insolvency power indexes are designed to reflect whether the supervisory authorities have been given the power to restructure, reorganise and declare a bank insolvent. The restructuring power index rates between 0 and 3, and the insolvency power index rates between 0 and 2. For both indexes higher values indicate greater power. Finally, the last column of Table 3.5 contains an evaluation of whether the regulator is an independent legal entity.

Table 3.5: Official supervisory variables in East Asia

	Super-visors per bank	Official super-visory power index	Prompt correc-tive action index	Restruc-turing power index	Insolv-ency power index	Indepen-dence of super-visory authority
Vietnam	3	11	0	3	2	no
Cambodia	0	13	5	3	2	no
China	1	11	3	3	2	yes
Indonesia	3	12	6	2	2	yes
Korea	6	9	4	3	2	no
Malaysia	5	n.a.	n.a.	3	2	no
Philippines	7	11	6	3	2	yes
Thailand	10	10	0	3	2	yes

Source: Calculated using information in Barth *et al.* (2001a, 2001b), and information from the World Bank office in Hanoi.

From Table 3.5 it can be seen that judging by the statues and legislation in place, the power of the supervisory authorities in Vietnam are on a par with the average for the region. Whether or not the regulator (the SBV) has the autonomy to actually enforce the laws is discussed in depth in Chapter 4.

Turning next to the power given to restructure and reorganise banks and to declare a troubled bank insolvent, it is found that the Vietnamese authorities are on average given with just as much power as the other countries in the region. However, when we turn

Table 3.6: Official supervisory variables in a global perspective

	Super-visors per bank	Official super-visory power	Prompt correc-tive power	Restruc-turing power	Declaring insolv-ency power	Inde-pendence of super-visory authority
Vietnam	3.0	11	0	3	2	no
Developed countries	0.94	11.08	1.19	2.50	1.27	n.a.
Developing countries	3.13	11.11	2.27	2.60	1.62	n.a.

Sources: Calculated using information in Barth *et al.* (2001a, 2001b) and information from the World Bank office in Hanoi.

to compare the prompt corrective power index (PCPI), it can be seen that the promptness by which the regulator can or will respond to problems in the financial sector is lower in Vietnam than in most other countries. This indicates problems from the supervisor's point of view when it comes to responding quickly to changes in the banking environment.

Table 3.6 indicates that the resources available as well as the legal rights bestowed upon a financial sector regulatory institution are lower in developing countries than in developed countries. This is no surprise. Table 3.6, however, also shows that Vietnamese financial regulation – with the important exception of the prompt corrective power – is on a par with or above the average for developing countries as a whole.

It would thus appear that while Vietnamese legislation is equal to or outperforms that of other countries of the region, the autonomy and power to rapidly implement these laws is lacking in Vietnam compared to the other countries in the region and in developing countries in general. Given that a swift regulatory response is a key determinant of the ability of a country to successfully avoid a financial instability this constitutes a serious shortcoming in the Vietnamese regulatory framework. The question of whether to give the SBV and their supervisors powers to act promptly was discussed in Vietnam during 2002, but the talks never materialised into actual legislation.

REGULATION OF BANKING ACTIVITIES

Tables 3.7 and 3.8 contain five indicators that measure of the degree of regulatory restrictiveness on the type of different activities banks can undertake. In each of the five a higher score implies a higher degree of restrictiveness (see Appendix C). As can be seen from Table 3.7, the banking sector in Vietnam is very restricted when it comes to the types of activities that banks are allowed to undertake.

Banks in Vietnam are generally prohibited from engaging in securities, insurance and real estate markets – activities that banks are allowed in the majority of the other countries in the region. Vietnam does not, however, differ much from neighbouring Cambodia or China. Vietnam is, however, on a par with the other countries in the region when it comes to the legislation governing ownership of banks and whether banks are allowed to own companies outside the sector.

The question of which activities banks should be allowed to undertake has generated considerable controversy and debate among financial sector specialists. One side argues that allowing for diversification of bank business operations may be beneficial because it makes it possible for banks to capitalise on synergies that originate from these complementary activities.

The competing, negative point of view identifies the following reasons for why it might be beneficial to restrict the degree to which banks can engage in diverse financial activities such as securities, insurance and real estate:

- Conflicts of interest may arise when banks engage in such diverse activities. Banks may, for example, attempt to dump securities on or shift risk to ill-informed investors so as to assist associated firms with outstanding loans.

- To the extent that moral hazard encourages riskier behaviour by banks, they will have more opportunities to increase risk if allowed to engage in a broader range of activities.

Table 3.7: Legal restrictions on banking activity in East Asia

	Securities activities	Insurance activities	Real Estate activities	Bank owning non-financial firms	Non-financial firms owning banks
Vietnam	4	4	4	2	3
Cambodia	4	4	4	2	1
China	4	3	4	3	4
Indonesia	2	4	4	4	1
Korea	2	2	2	3	3
Malaysia	2	2	3	3	3
Philippines	1	2	2	2	3
Thailand	2	2	2	3	3

Sources: Calculated using information in Barth *et al.* (2001a, 2001b) and information from the World Bank office in Hanoi.

Table 3.8: Legal restrictions on banking activity in a global perspective

	Securities activities	Insurance activities	Real estate activities	Bank owning non-financial firms	Non-financial firms owning banks
Vietnam	4.00	4.00	4.00	2.00	3.00
Developed countries	1.37	2.22	2.04	2.22	1.77
Developing countries	2.04	2.90	3.19	2.53	2.13

Sources: Calculated using information in Barth *et al.* (2001a, 2001b) and information from the World Bank office in Hanoi.

- Broad financial activities and the mixing of banking and commerce may lead to the formation of extremely large and complex entities that are extraordinarily difficult to monitor.

- Large institutions may become so politically and economically powerful that it becomes very difficult (if not impossible) to discipline them.

- Large financial conglomerates may reduce competition and hence the efficiency potential of the sector.

Since the theoretical discussion remains unsettled, one inevitably turns to empirical analyses to see whether a clearer conclusion emerges here. The cross-country work by Barth *et al.* (2001a) finds that restricting banking activities is negatively associated with bank development. Restricting banks from engaging in securities activities is also strongly negatively associated with bank development. Finally, the diversification of income sources through non-traditional bank activities is generally positively associated with bank stability, especially in economies with active non-bank financial markets.

One explanation for these findings is that the exploitation of economies of scale *is* in fact beneficial to the development and stability of the financial sector. Furthermore, it can be argued that banks have the incentive to behave prudently if fewer regulatory restrictions increase their franchise value. Another possible explanation is that a diversified income stream creates more stable banks. Finally, one could argue that high levels of government restrictions promote government power, and thereby (perhaps) create a bigger role for corruption, hindering bank performance and stability. While this is speculative, one has to admit that the results from and the discussion about the results by Barth *et al.* indicate that it may be worthwhile considering liberalising the laws regarding those activities in which Vietnamese banks are allowed to engage.

SAFETY NETS AND CAPITAL ADEQUACY

Safety net policies are designed to address the potential fragility of financial systems, including the prevention of bank runs and bank failures.[5] In short, safety nets are designed to reduce the incentives for banks to take risks and lessen depositors' incentives to withdraw their funds. The existence of such insurance mechanisms can, however, have an adverse effect on risk-taking incentives. The presence of a deposit insurance scheme may, for example, lead depositors to disregard the risks of bank failure. Instead of evaluating whether a bank can actually deliver the promised high interest rates on deposits, the insured depositors will only look at the level of interest rate when choosing a bank.

Tables 3.9 and 3.10 list a number of variables describing the level and nature of capital regulation. The methodology used to construct these indicators is described in Appendix C. Generally, higher values indicate greater stringency. Looking at Tables 3.9 and 3.10, it appears that Vietnam has very restrictive requirements regarding the amount of capital that a bank must have compared to other countries in the region. The capital regulatory index for Vietnam is more in line with what is observed in developed countries than in developing countries.

Table 3.9: Capital regulatory variables in East Asia

	Overall capital stringency (0–6)	Initial capital stringency (0–3)	Capital regulatory index (0–9)
Vietnam	5	1	6
Cambodia	3	1	4
China	n.a.	3	n.a.
Indonesia	2	3	5
Korea	5	1	6
Malaysia	1	2	3
Philippines	2	1	3
Thailand	3	2	5

Sources: Calculated using information in Barth *et al.* (2001a, 2001b), information from the World Bank office in Hanoi and The Banking Legislation in Vietnam Decree No. 166/1999/ND-CP (SBV, 2000).

Table 3.10: Capital regulatory variables in a global perspective

	Overall capital stringency (0–6)	Initial capital stringency (0–3)	Capital regulatory index (0–9)
Vietnam	5.00	1.00	6.00
Developed countries	4.19	1.85	6.08
Developing countries	3.20	1.46	4.65

Sources: Calculated using information in Barth *et al.* (2001a, 2001b), information from the World Bank office in Hanoi and The Banking Legislation in Vietnam Decree No. 166/1999/ND-CP (SBV, 2000).

From a theoretical point of view, regulation of capital adequacy can have both positive and negative effects on financial development. Capital requirements may serve as an incentive against engaging in high-risk activities. Yet negative effects may occur due to the difficulties of regulators and supervisors in setting capital standards that mimic those that would be demanded by well-informed private market participants.

Looking at the empirical evidence in this area, Barth *et al.* (2001a) find no robust relationship between capital regulatory restrictiveness and bank development. Furthermore the relationship between the stringency of official capital requirements and the likelihood of a crisis is not strong.

As described above, safety nets that are designed to deal with the potential problems facing financial systems are often subject to critisism and have in many countries been identified as one of the sources of financial fragility (World Bank 2002). Deposit insurance encourages excessive risk-taking behaviour in countries where the relevant regulation and supervision to counter such behaviour has not yet been fully developed. In addition, badly designed safety nets can undermine the incentives of the participants in the financial system. On the other hand deposit insurance schemes provide protection. For example, if too many depositors attempt to withdraw their funds at once, an illiquid but solvent bank can fail.

Barth *et al.* (2001a) do not find a strong link between the generosity of the deposit insurance system and bank development. They do, on the other hand, find a very strong link between the generosity of the deposit insurance system and bank sector fragility. This result is consistent with the view that deposit insurance not only substantially aggravates problems of moral hazard but also produces deleterious effects on bank fragility. The results suggest that the reverse incentive effects from deposit insurance may overwhelm the stabilising effects that these safety nets may also have. Given these results, it is not clear that the implementation of a deposit insurance design in the Vietnamese financial sector would have beneficial effects on bank development.

CONCLUDING REMARKS

Analysing the competitive pressure in the Vietnamese financial sector, it was found that although Vietnam in recent years has levelled the playing field for new entrants somewhat, there is still much to be done before the Vietnamese banking environment can be characterised as competitive or even partly competitive for that matter.

Given that bank concentration in Vietnam coincides with state ownership, one option would be to strengthen the already initiated efforts to equitise the SOCBs. This is, however, a lengthy process that is unlikely to proceed unless the problems of non-performing loans and continued policy lending are resolved (see Chapter 4). Current thinking in Vietnam is that the equitisation of the SOCBs will not be piloted before 2006 at the earliest.

Another approach is to making financial markets more contestable – i.e. increase the competition between banks already in the sector. The USBTA ensures that this process will accelerate in the coming years. In this context, the concerns about the risk of 'unhealthy competition' among the SOCBs made in the recent World Bank Banking Sector Review (World Bank 2002) should perhaps be reconsidered. The Vietnamese banking sector is characterised by so little inter-bank competition that any indirect regulation with the objective of making SOCBs 'stay within the areas assigned to them during the period of central planning' is likely to make the eventual entry of foreign banks resemble shock therapy.

Any attempt to introduce new entrants and a higher level of competitiveness in the sector should of course be gradual so that the franchise value of local banks does not erode quickly, causing instability and increased risk of financial crises. As a consequence, any liberalisation of the entry process must be managed over time and transparent. Prior to opening the sector to new and most likely more sophisticated entrants, the Vietnamese government must, however, strengthen the capacity and autonomy of the regulatory framework. The regional comparison presented in this chapter points to several areas that need attention.

The promptness by which the regulator can or will respond to problems in the financial sector is generally lower in Vietnam than in the other countries in the region. Hence, while Vietnamese legislation is equal to or outperforms that of other countries in the region, the autonomy and power to rapidly implement these laws is lacking in Vietnam compared to these other countries in the region. Moreover, the Vietnamese banking system appears to be very restricted when looking at the types of activities banks can engage in. Banks in Vietnam are generally prohibited from engaging in securities, insurance and real estate markets – activities that are permitted or only somewhat restricted in most other countries in the region. Finally, it was found that Vietnam compared to the countries in the region has very restrictive requirements regarding the amount of capital that a bank must have.

NOTES

1   This explains the recent (and the present) focus on financial sector regulation and supervision.

2   The analysis of financial services to the agricultural sector presented in Chapter 5 will cover this in more detail.

3   Note, however, that it is not necessarily evident that a causal relationship exists between the entry of a foreign bank and the subsequent exit of a domestic bank. If, for example, the domestic bank was burdened by a high ratio of non-performing loans caused by failed lending in the past, one might just as well say these past failures

caused the domestic bank to fail. In this case the entry of foreign banks would have revealed a problem rather than created it.

4   The methodology used by Barth *et al.* (2001) to construct the indicators used in this chapter is presented in Appendix C.

5   The development of a deposit insurance scheme in Vietnam was discussed in Chapter 2.

CHAPTER 4

The State Bank of Vietnam

The State Bank of Vietnam (the SBV) holds a central position in both the day-to-day workings of the financial sector and in the plans to reform it. This position rests in part upon the significance and powers bestowed upon the central bank, and in part on the informal of structures and procedures that have remained in place from the period prior to the Doi Moi reforms. More specifically, the Vietnamese tradition of consensus governance, in combination with government concerns with maintaining social and political stability, continues to exert considerable influence on the SBV (see Chapter 1).

As a consequence, the transformation of the former monobank into a fully independent two-tiered banking system is still ongoing. This can be viewed as a dual process of separation. On one side the SBV has to some extent already been separated from actual banking operations in order to focus on supervision and control of financial institutions and markets and the management of money and credit aggregates. On the other side, the SBV also has to be separated from the political system in order to operate as an autonomous entity on a par with the executive, legislative and judiciary branches of government. As will be shown in this chapter, this second process of separation has yet to begin in full.

Although Chapters 2 and 3 outlined several areas of persistent and significant government influence on both the commercial banking system and the SBV, the analysis presented in the next section will look at SBV autonomy in greater detail. The following section will describe and discuss SBV management of key financial markets, after which a look will be taken at SBV supervision and regulation of the financial markets. The final section will discuss the issue of non-performing loans in the banking system and the measures implemented by the SBV to resolve these loans.

THE INDEPENDENCE OF THE SBV

Central bank independence is an old principle among economists and practitioners of monetary policy whose support has fluctuated considerably over time. In this context, a key debate is whether and when to push for an independent central bank in a developing country. One school of thought, starting with Rogoff (1985) has pointed out that a conservative and politically independent central bank is necessary to reduce the inflationary bias resulting from the time inconsistency problem first analysed by Kydland and Prescott (1977). The time inconsistency problem arises if policymakers are able to persuade the public of the credibility of a certain inflationary target and the public behaves accordingly. In this case, a government facing an election will have an incentive to create an unexpected expansion of the monetary base. This expansion will in turn lead to lower unemployment (the benefit anticipated by the government) and subsequently higher inflation. The rise in inflation is, however, likely to occur with a lag and will therefore only occur after the government expects to have been re-elected on account of their success in managing the economy. The higher level of inflation can thus be viewed as the price the government is prepared to pay to secure re-election. If, however, the public is aware of these in-centives (i.e. can form rational expectations), it will take into account that the government will deviate from the announced inflationary target. The higher inflationary expectations held by the public subsequently leave the government with little choice but to validate these expectations. Hence, in the simple model described above, aggregate output will be the same whether or not the government deviates from the announced inflationary target, whereas the level of inflation will be above what it would have been had the government stuck to its rule. Both the government and the public have a common interest in avoiding this suboptimal outcome. The problem is that even if the government intends to stick to the announced target of low inflation – i.e. restricts the temptation to loosen monetary policy facing an election – this will not be credible to the public. As a consequence, high inflationary expectations will be formed regardless of the government's true intentions and announcements.

The solution pointed out by Rogoff and others is for the government to disengage from its control of monetary policy by creating a conservative central bank responsible for price stability. Thereby the government effectively ties its own hands in order for the public to attach credibility to the commitment to low inflation. While empirical evidence appears to support a negative relationship between central bank independence and inflation in the OECD,[1] the empirical evidence is less clear when it comes to developing countries. Using the turnover rate of central bank governors as an incomplete proxy for central bank independence, de Haan and Kooi (2000) find that central bank independence is only related to inflation when high inflation countries (i.e. where annual inflation exceeds 300 per cent) are included in their sample of 82 developing countries.

Others have pointed to the possibility of reverse causality. This would correspond to the situation where low levels of inflation (although perhaps not attributable to the central bank) will make the central bank more reputable. This in turn will allow the central bank to seek and secure greater autonomy.

The ambiguous empirical evidence and the possibility of reverse causality coupled with the fact that legal independence seldom corresponds to political independence has given rise to a competing school of thought concerning the benefits of central bank independence. Here, the central claim is that central bank independence is overstressed and that the problems involved with building an independent central bank have been overlooked (see, for example, Mas 1995). Leading proponents of this view such as Goodman (1991) and Posen (1994) argue that developing countries should not embark on the difficult and lengthy process of trying to create a legally and politically independent central bank. Instead, they should try to create and strengthen a domestic constituency for low inflation. Among the staunchest members of such an anti-inflation constituency would be private banks, which due to the maturity mismatch of their assets and liabilities and the nonmarketable nature of assets are particularly vulnerable to high inflation.

The idea that creating favourable conditions for the establishment of private banks will lead to a more independent central bank through higher outside pressure for low inflation could be described as an indirect approach. This rival school of thought may help to explain why empirical studies fail to find a robust negative correlation between central bank independence and inflation in developing countries. The reason (according to Goodman and Posen) is that the private banking sector is relatively small in these countries, resulting in the anti-inflation constituencies being relatively small and without political clout.

According to this school of thought governments should not waste energy and reputation trying to create an independent central bank, whose autonomy they are more likely to violate themselves at a later stage of crisis. Instead, the government should opt for a process of building a base of support for lower inflation outside the policy environment. This can take place through a deregulation and privatisation of the financial sector, thereby creating anti-inflationary institutions external to the government. As it would be difficult for a government to exercise extensive control or roll back private bank-ing sector once it is established, this approach essentially also amounts to the government tying its own hands in order to achieve more credibility.

Prior to a discussion of whether a direct or an indirect approach to obtaining central bank independence is best suited to the Vietnamese context, the analysis will evaluate the present level of SBV independence. But how can measure central bank independence be measured? Hermes and Lensink (2000) introduce the following examples of typologies/methods used to identify different aspects of central bank independence:

- **Political vs economic independence.** According to Grilli *et al.* (1991), political independence refers to the degree to which a central bank can independently pursue a goal of price stability, while economic independence seeks to uncover the degree to which the central bank autonomously can determine the terms and conditions of credit to the central government. The distinction between political and economic independence is subsequently used to analyse the degree of central bank independence *vis-à-vis* key central bank policy objectives.

- **Goal vs instrument independence.** First introduced by Debelle and Fischer (1994), goal independence refers to the extent to which the central bank can set its own policy goals and objectives. Instrument independence reflects the degree to which the central bank is able to freely choose and assign policy instruments to obtain a given goal.

- **Legal vs actual independence.** This distinction was introduced by Cukierman (1992). Here, legal independence refers to the degree of independence stipulated in the laws governing the central bank, whereas actual independence is the political independence that results from the interpretation and/or circumvention of these laws.

For the purpose of this analysis, the approach suggested by Cukierman appears the best suited. However, to take into account that actual independence as defined by Cukierman may be affected by factors that are both internal and external to the SBV, a third type of independence, termed 'operational independence' will be added. The result is the following three types of independence: (i) legal independence defined as the degree of independence stipulated in the laws about the SBV; (ii) political independence defined as the actual practice and whether or not this corresponds to what is stipulated by the legislation, and (iii) operational independence defined as the ability to design and implement policies and strategies. The last is primarily assessed by looking at the human capital in the SBV as well as the strategies in place to attract, augment, and further develop the human capital available.[2]

Thus, the difference between political and operational independence is that the former looks at factors that are predominantly external to the SBV, whereas the latter focuses on constraints that are internal to the SBV. The three forms of independence should be regarded as non-substitutable and necessary if the SBV is to function as a functionally independent central bank. The three forms will in turn be considered below.

In terms of legislation, the Law on the State Bank is the principal reference and the first legal confirmation of the independence of the SBV.[3] Here and in the law on credit institutions it was stipulated and affirmed that interference in the lawful operations of the state bank and credit institutions is prohibited. While this clearly represents an important legal confirmation of the independence of the SBV, its significance can only be evaluated in combination with the actual powers bestowed upon the SBV in the same context. Here, the Law on the State Bank stipulates that the SBV is only responsible for the formulation of a national monetary policy. The policies formulated by the SBV are subsequently submitted to the government for consideration. The government then submits the perhaps modified national monetary policy to the National Assembly for approval. The SBV does not have the final word and is not the last to make decisions on issues concerning the national monetary policy. Thus, in comparison with some countries where the central banks are not tied to the government, like the Fed in the United States and the Bundesbank of Germany, the legal degree of independence of the SBV is restricted.

As for the power to make decisions concerning future plans and to conduct monetary and credit policy, the SBV is also subject to the direction of the government and in some cases interference by local authorities. Although the powers and duties of these offices are restricted, the operations of the municipal and provincial branches of the SBV are frequently interfered with and/or disrupted by local authorities. The management of foreign exchange reserves and the usage of foreign exchange reserves also have to conform to government requirements.

In addition, the legal powers bestowed upon the SBV in terms of supervisory activities related to restructuring and reorganising banks were considered and compared with those of other countries in the region in Chapter 3. Although it was found that the SBV on average has been granted greater powers than those of other developing countries, the SBV supervisors are not allowed to take prompt actions when irregularities are detected. The law does not, for example, establish predetermined levels of bank solvency deterioration that force automatic actions. As a consequence, the promptness by which the SBV can or will respond to problems in the financial sector is lower in Vietnam than in most other countries in the region.[4] Finally, the regional comparison found that the supervisory authorities in the SBV have no or low independence from Vietnamese officials, but that this did not differ significantly from the situation in the other countries in the region.

Turning to the possibilities accorded by the legislation for the SBV to act as an independent supervisor of the financial sector, the Law on the State Bank states that the department of banking supervision is to be headquartered at the State Bank of Vietnam. The department is to advise the SBV governor on implementing state management and the functions of the central bank. The SBV supervision is to be directed by the guidelines of the state inspector in co-ordination with the Banking Operation Centre of the SBV. However, unlike the directors of other departments in the SBV, who are appointed by the SBV governor, the chief of banking supervision is appointed by the prime minister according to recommendations from the SBV governor and general chief of the state inspector.[5] As a consequence, the bank supervision department enjoys less independence than other departments of the state bank. If, for example, the SBV governor does not agree with the dispositions made by the chief of banking supervision, the latter will still be able to execute his/her plans, although the chief of banking supervision is also responsible to the SBV governor for assigned tasks.

Overall, the level of legal independence of the SBV is mixed. A comparison with, for example, OECD countries would indicate that the Vietnamese central bank in many respects is still is a body of the government, while a comparison with the other countries in the region and developing countries in general would indicate that the level of legal independence of the SBV in a number of areas is on a par with or exceeds that which is observed in these countries. The lack of legally stipulated powers to react promptly to violations of the existing legislation is, however, a serious shortcoming. Another such shortcoming is the SBV's lack of real decision power when it comes to the design of monetary policies.

Following the approach introduced by Cukierman (1992), political central bank independence can be approximated by the average turnover rate (TOR) of central bank governors. Possibly due to the fact that it can be measured and compared across countries, the TOR of central bank governors has become one of the most widely used and cited indicators of actual (political) central bank independence. Table 4.1 compares the TOR of central bank governors in Vietnam with that of other countries in the region.

Table 4.1: Turnover rate of central bank governors (annual average)

	1980–89	1990–98
Indonesia	0.20	0.25
Korea	0.40	0.50
Malaysia	0.20	0.25
Singapore	0.30	0.25
Thailand	0.10	0.75
Vietnam*	0.33	0.50

Note: The list of Vietnamese central bank governors since 1980 is: Tran Doung (1980–82); Nguyen Duygia (1982–86); Lu Minh Chau (1986–89); Cao Sy Kien (1989–97); Do Que Luong (1997–98); Nguyen Tan Dung (1998–2000); and Le Duc Thuy (2000–).
Sources: Sturm and de Haan (2001) and CIEM

Table 4.1 indicates that the level of political independence of the SBV is relatively low compared to what its regional counterparts enjoy. In addition, the level of independence has fallen over the two periods for which regional data are available. This corresponds with the above observations that the autonomy of the SBV decreased with the passing of the State Bank Law in 1998.

The conclusions derived from looking at Table 4.1 should, however, not be overemphasised. Using the TOR as an indicator for political central bank independence is not without problems. First, a change of central bank governor might be caused by a multitude of reasons not necessarily related to unduly and excessive central government interference. Second, a central bank governor may remain in office for a long time because he/she is acquiescing in government wishes and priorities. Third, the usefulness of the measure rests upon the assumption that some conflict of interest exists between the central bank governor and the government. As the description of the system of consensus governance in Chapter 1 has made clear, this need not be the case in Vietnam.

As pointed out by Klump and Gottwald (2003) the SBV governor has to remain a member of the government following his appointment. Hence, Nguyen Tan Dung, who was elected in 1998, continued to function as deputy prime minister of Vietnam and as a member of the Central Committee of the Communist Party. Likewise, the current SBV governor, Le Duc Thuy, is also still a member of both the government and the Central Committee. Hence, if anything, the use of the TOR to measure the actual level of political independence might actually overestimate it.

Another indication of the limited political independence of the SBV is the fact that the SBV is still required to report to the government for approval of matters that have been left for the SBV to decide. Regulations that should have been promulgated as decisions of the governor of the state bank but were promulgated as decrees of the Government bear testimony to this type of influence. Consequently, the overall assessment of the level of SBV political independence is that the SBV, in accordance with the Vietnamese tradition of consensus governance, relies extensively on guidance and consent from the government. Although the SBV in some areas is independent by statute, it will nevertheless accept that the consensus agreement formed through consultations with the government and/or the Central Committee of the Communist Party will prevail regardless of the rules.

Turning to an assessment of the operational independence of the SBV, it is necessary to look more closely at personnel and training issues. The total number of staff at the SBV is between 6,500 and 7,000. The central office in Hanoi employs 800 people. Some 60, 100, 70, and 30 to 50 people are employed in the Department of Monetary Policy, the State Bank's Inspection Division, the Technology Department and other departments, respectively. Remaining staff work in the 61 municipal and provincial branches and the representative offices. Movement of staff between the central state bank and municipal and provincial branches in management and operation of the system is generally not recommended by the SBV.

Some of the municipal and provincial branches appear to be overstaffed compared to assigned functions and duties.[6] The problem of overstaffing is a recurring issue, which the SBV has not been able to solve. This is primarily due to obstacles resulting from the personnel policy of the state.

The training of SBV staff is undertaken by the Banking Institute. At present, the Banking Institute has one sub-institute in Ho Chi Minh City and seven faculties and a dozen special departments in Hanoi. Annually, the Banking Institute selects and trains about 2,000 students and thousands of short-term apprentices as well as some 20 graduate students. The curriculum taught and the qualifications of the lecturers at the Banking Institute are, however, not comparable with those found in Vietnamese universities, and the State Bank has expressed concern about the quality and applicability of the training given. Thus, although the annual number of staff trained is large, the quality of the training provided has not met the internal requirements. In addition, the present general promotion scheme appears to be based on seniority rather than skills and qualifications.

In conclusion, the operational independence of the SBV appears to be restricted by an organisational structure that permits overstaffing, especially at the municipal and provincial offices. Operational independence is further hampered by the insufficient quality and applicability of the training received in internal training institutions.

Overall, it must be concluded that the SBV with its current capacity cannot effectively develop and execute national monetary policies. The SBV remains operationally and politically dependent upon support from other government agencies. One could therefore question whether the more restrictive Law on the State Bank is the binding constraint. Given that the SBV in a number of cases refrains from making decisions that are clearly within its area of jurisdiction and competence, it would appear more likely that lack of political independence is more binding. It is thus unlikely that attempts to further separate the SBV from the government though direct legislative channels will bring much change. As a consequence, the more indirect route of gradually building and strengthening a non-governmental lobby for an independent central bank might be more of a prospect. The preliminary plans for the equitisation of the large state-owned banks represent an important step in this direction, as does the expected increased presence of foreign banks due to the USBTA and the Vietnamese bid for WTO membership. The current low levels of inflation imply that anti-inflation (as suggested by Posen (1994) and Mas (1995)) is unlikely to become a common cause under which a private lobby would unite. However, other pressing issues such as increased transparency, adherence to international auditing standards and/or less government interference readily present themselves as possible unifying themes for a future private lobby.

While this is clearly a long-term process, the short-term priority could be to identify and describe the status, role, and functions of the SBV in more detail. A comprehensive assessment of the implementation of functions and duties of the SBV under the Law on State Bank (1998) is currently under way. This is expected to form the basis for a comprehensive plan to reorganise the SBV, perhaps resulting in increased SBV autonomy. Given the prevailing political and economic environment in Vietnam, following a more gradual, indirect route towards increasing central bank independence appears to be the most productive and effective approach – also in the short to medium term.

SBV MANAGEMENT AND CONTROL OF SELECTED FINANCIAL MARKETS

Among their principal tasks all central banks have to ensure the stability and development of the payment system and the banking sector. One way in which the central bank can hope to achieve these is by ensuring and facilitating the development of key markets for financial services and products, thereby giving agents and institutions the choice between financial products that vary in terms, conditions and liquidity. This section will focus on to what extent and how the SBV facilitates the markets for bonds[7] and the inter-bank market for domestic and foreign currency.

As pointed out by Herring and Chatusripitak (2000), financial sector analysts have paid comparatively little attention to role of the bond market. In the case of East Asia this lack of attention can be explained (but not justified) by the relatively small role played by the bond market as a source of capital and point of reference for financial markets in the region. There are, however, a number of good reasons to take a closer look at the bond market and the implications that the absence of such a market can have on the financial sector.

First, the absence of a market for government bonds implies that the economy will not have a yield curve that depicts the market-determined term structure of interest rates reflecting the opportunity cost of funds at different maturities. As the yield curve for government bonds is used to price the term structure of more risky assets, the lack of a benchmark bond is likely to cause mispricing and inefficiencies in other areas of the financial sector.[8] One reason is that the lack of perceived safe benchmark investment means that it becomes more difficult for investors to form expectations over the future earnings of an investment project and to discount these accordingly.

Second, the underdevelopment of a bond market leaves savers with a choice between investing their savings in real assets (real estate, gold or land) and depositing them in banks. If trust in the banking system is low, fewer deposits are mobilised for productive investments.

Third, the lack of a government benchmark implies that it will be very difficult if not impossible for firms to use corporate bonds as a source of investment. Instead, firms will have to use the stock market (if it is developed) or turn to domestic[9] banks for financing. The comparatively small stock markets in many developing countries have the result that banks often represent the sole source of outside funding for firms.

Fourth, due to the absence of government bonds domestic financial institutions are precluded from issuing their own bonds, which might reduce their exposure to liquidity risks. This has implications for, for example, life insurance companies and pension funds which will find it more difficult to acquire assets that match the maturity of their liabilities.

Of all these factors, the lack of information presented by a yield curve on government bonds is perhaps the most severe problem. The lack of a clear indication of the opportunity cost of capital at different maturities makes it very difficult to make investment decisions. In this context it should, of course, be noted that a yield curve on government bonds will decrease considerably or even be worthless if the government tries to manipulate the bond market in order to lower the cost of government borrowing.

The market for government bonds is still nascent in Vietnam. According to the World Bank (2002b), the government has for some time been now issuing government bonds and notes for the domestic market. The buyers are primarily the insurance companies and the SOCBs, who use the bonds as collateral when utilising the SBV discount and refinancing windows.

It appears that the government primarily views the issuance of bonds as a means to finance deficits, disregarding the role of the bond market in forwarding the development of a market-based financial sector. Financing budget deficits is, of course, the primary reason for why governments issue bonds, but it is important to note that issuing bonds to finance a budget deficit does not preclude governments from trying at the same time to facilitate financial sector development through the creation of a market-determined yield curve.[10] Failure to consider this dual objective severely undermines the usefulness of a yield curve on government bonds as a benchmark for maturity pricing of equities. In addition, the issuance of government bonds does not appear to be coordinated with that of the SBV, possibly resulting in confusion and unnecessary fluctuations that may restrict the development of markets for both types of debt instrument.

Taking a closer look at the market for treasury bills highlights some of the problems still facing the development of a market for government bonds. In Vietnam, treasury bills are issued via three channels: the SBV, municipal and provincial branches of the treasury and the stock exchange. Up to now, data on the total value of T-bills and bond issues through municipal and provincial branches of the Treasury have not been published. However, indications are that this amount is not large. The total amount of T-bills issued through the stock exchange is also small. As a result, T-bills and bonds are still only traded when issued directly by the SBV. Table 4.2 depicts the development of funds mobilised through T-bills bidding.

Table 4.2: The market for treasury bills

	1995	1996	1997	1998	2000
Total amount (billion dong)	243	967	2913	4,020.7	4,766
Number of auctions (units)	4	19	37	44	46
Average interest rate per year (%)	17.2-18	7.9-13.8	9–11.3	11.6-11.4	5.2

Source: State Bank of Vietnam

The introduction of open-market operations as an instrument of monetary policy in 1998 was considered an important component of the overall financial sector reforms. The initial results obtained in the three-year period in which open-market operations have been conducted allow for cautious optimism. In the two years from July 2000 up there were 73 transactions totalling 8,116 billion dong.

One can identify a number of restrictions to the development and growth of the secondary market for treasury bills and government bonds. These include the fact that only T-bills and SBV bills are traded in the market, and that only short-term value trades (shorter than one year) are allowed in the market. This may hinder the development of a secondary market as potential participants may find it difficult to obtain a desired level of risk and asset diversification.

The number of participants who met the conditions to enter the market for treasury bills in 2000 was 22. In reality only eight credit institutions made transactions; among these, it was mainly the four large state-owned commercial banks. The relatively small size of the market in combination with the fact that the majority of the buyers were government-controlled institutions indicates that the market was still lacking both depth (defined as the quantity that can be sold without moving prices against the seller) and breadth (defined as the heterogeneity of the participants and their likely responses to new information). Hence, the plan to use open-market operations as a key instrument of monetary policy still appears to be rather ambitious. The result could be a vicious circle where legal/administrative restrictions prevent the market from growing and the limited size of the market results in a lack of pressure for legal changes and/or limited attention to the problem by the responsible legislative bodies.

According to persistent rumours, the Ministry of Finance has been preparing a draft proposal to issue an internationally traded series of government bonds during 2004. Although not directly related to the SBV role as a creator and facilitator of markets, there is good reason to pause and consider possible implications of a decision to go ahead. The preliminary assessment in 2003 was that the Ministry of Finance was to issue a total of 500 million dollars in seven-year Eurobonds. Subsequent talks, however, indicate that the final amount could be significantly lower, or that the issuance might be dropped altogether. Various arguments can be identified to explain why the government found it relevant to consider issuing international bonds:

1. Any funds raised would provide a welcome supplement to existing sources of government funding.

2. Such an action could provide a much needed benchmark for setting interest rate levels in Vietnam. This would serve to improve the framework and conditions for the other bonds and T-bills issued by the government and the SBV.

3. The successful maintenance of an international series of Euro bonds would provide a clear signal to international investors that Vietnam is moving decisively and competently in the direction of increased reliance on market forces. Such a signal

could in the long run improve the country's chances of attracting foreign direct investments.

4. It would also constitute an important signal to the domestic market that the country was similar to the other East Asian economies – hence contributing to government's strategy of holding on to power by maintaining their 'performance legitimacy'.

5. Finally, it would make it easier for Vietnamese banks (primarily the SOCBs) to attract funds from abroad, as the bond interest rate would provide a benchmark to which a bank-specific risk-premium can be added.

One can, however, also identify a number of related concerns. First, there is a potential risk that the government's commitment towards the international financial market would 'raise eyebrows' in the donor community. Donors may find it harder to justify giving concessional loans and/or international development assistance to countries that can attract international capital on market terms. Second, opening a series of international bonds can entail a potential risk of contagion in the event of a new regional crisis. Analyses of the East Asian financial crisis have indicated that an element of financial contagion was at play in the transformation of the crisis from an internal problem in Malaysia to a regional crisis. More specifically, herd behaviour by international investors who continued to perceive the East Asian economies as a bloc were to some degree to blame for this (Park and Lee 2002). By linking domestic interest rate fixation to the bond series, Vietnam would open a potential backdoor for future financial crises as this policy could cause domestic interest rates to rise with the rates on the international bond. Another problem could arise if the market for Vietnamese government bonds fails to achieve sufficient depth,[11] potentially making the fixation of interest rates volatile and more susceptible to runs and speculative arbitrage.

These problems could, of course, be avoided by abstaining from using the bond rate as an anchor, thereby effectively maintaining an almost complete isolation of the domestic financial market. A decision to isolate the Eurobond from the domestic financial market would, however, mean that the much needed benchmark for domestic interest rates is lost and that the signal value of issuing international bonds is lessened. Such a decision would be likely to have a detrimental effect upon the credibility of the on-going financial reforms, which in turn could make the bond less attractive to international investors.

Finally, opening up for increased domestic borrowing abroad raises the long-run complexity of how to sequence future financial sector liberalisation. Maintaining a closed capital account and a fixed exchange rate while increasing the amount of dollar-denominated loans in Vietnamese banks represents a real risk. If a future decision to open the capital account results in pressure on the dong, the government could face a situation where the consequences of defending the dong and letting it float would both be detrimental. Recent research into the East Asian Financial Crisis indicates that a deterioration of firm balance sheets following the first wave of devaluations was one of the factors augmenting the crisis. More specifically, companies with large dollar-denominated loans saw their balance sheets deteriorate as a result of the devaluations in the first phase of the EAFC. The problems of these companies in turn caused problems for the domestic banks, thereby creating a vicious circle that reinforced the crisis.

Whether or not the Vietnamese government will press ahead with the issuing of international bonds is inevitably a political decision, but as the above discussion has made clear, it is important to consider the implications for the entire sector and the ongoing financial reforms.

The inter-bank market for domestic currency transactions was established in a rudimentary form in 1993 in an attempt to strengthen the role of the SBV in monetary management (World Bank 1995). The governor of the State Bank of Vietnam established a firmer legal basis for the market by issuing Decision 132 in July 1998. Here it was stipulated that the inter-bank domestic currency market (IDCM) was to be organised and regulated by the State Bank to assist credit institutions in making an effective use of their capital and ensuring their capacity to meet payment obligations.

The SBV consequently has the 'dual' role of market regulator and market member. In order to be allowed to participate, commercial banks have to meet a range of stipulated conditions. These include having an account in the Trade Office of the State Bank, having a representative at the Transaction Centre of the IDCM and having an internal informational system linking the headquarters to the Transaction Centre.

According to the status of the IDCM, two types of lending activities are allowed in this market: borrowing to cover a deficit in clearing payments and borrowing to extend a credit (short-term lending). All transactions are carried out in dong. This rule also applies to branches of foreign banks and joint-venture banks. As foreign banks still face restrictions on the domestic-currency-gathering activities, this market has become their primary source of funding (Klump and Gottwald 2003).

If a credit institution does not have enough funds to carry out clearing payments, it can borrow from the branch of the State Bank where it has opened its account, but only for a maturity of up to 10 days. The member banks may repay their debt to the State Bank before the term of payment at any time, but earlier repayment to other members is accepted only if these agree.

To link and solve the demand–supply relationship for foreign exchange among credit institutions, Vietnam established an inter-bank foreign-exchange market. This was first established in October 1994. Up to 1997, there were 58 participants in the market. The annual transaction volume of foreign exchange among credit institutions was US$ 720 million. The transaction volume among credit institutions increased following Decision 37 on accelerating management of foreign exchange and Decision 173 on the obligation of sale and rights to buy for resident organisations, as well as adjustments in foreign exchange-rate circulation. The market, however, remains without depth (World Bank 2002). As already mentioned in Chapter 2, the East Asian Crisis almost caused the market to shut down as the daily volume of transactions dropped from US$ 8 million to below US$ 200,000.

SBV REGULATION AND SUPERVISION OF THE FINANCIAL SECTOR

Whether or not the supervision and regulation of the financial sector is among the core tasks of a central bank can be discussed.

Some analysts like Beckerman (1997) argue that the tasks of managing credit, money and foreign-reserve aggregates are formidable and that central bank directors should focus on these while leaving supervision to a specialised supervisory institution. The underlying argument is twofold. First, reference is made to a (perceived) resource constraint on management[12] capacity. The argument is that supervision is likely to take up the time and attention of central bank directors, giving them less time to focus on the above core tasks. Second, the inclusion of supervision and regulation among central bank tasks could give rise to potential conflicts of interests and possible problems of moral hazard. Central bank directors could, for example, feel tempted to ease overall money and credit policies inappropriately in order to ease their own supervision task.

Analysts like Hermes and Lensink (2000) disagree and argue that bank supervision is inherently a central bank function as it assists in maintaining and safeguarding the overall stability of the system.

This divergence of views is also reflected in actual differences in central bank practice across countries. Some central banks like the US Federal Reserve Bank regard supervision of the financial sector to be among its core tasks, while others, like, for example, the Danish central bank have delegated the task to an independent supervisory institution. Moreover, no norm or set of guidelines analogous to the commercial banks' Basel norms exist for central banks.

In Vietnam, the question of whether the SBV should undertake the supervision and regulation of the sector is only just beginning to attract attention, and we will return to consider this question towards the end of this section. First it will, however, be useful to turn to a description of how the SBV conducts its supervision. This will be followed by the identification and discussion of some of the problems in this area.

Banking supervision did (as pointed out in Chapter 1) only exist to a limited degree in the former monobank system. It was only after the Law on the State Bank in 1998 that steps were taken to ensure a legal foundation for banking supervision. The Law of the State Bank is, however, no longer the sole law guiding banking supervision. Banking supervision has been made subject to the law on credit institutions and other regulations, including ordinances on inspection, ordinances on resisting corruption, the law on complaint accusation and ordinances on penalising administrative violations.

The Law of the State Bank, however, remains the most important legal basis for SBV supervision. Table 4.3 summarises the situation before and after the Law on the State Bank. As can be seen from the table, the Law on the State Bank stipulated both the responsibilities, purpose and objects of SBV supervision, and must as such be described as an important step in the development of the financial sector. On an organisational level, banking supervision at the SBV includes offices for each of the dominant types of bank (SOCBs, JSBs and foreign banks). Separate SBV divisions handle analysis, inspection and the treatment of complaints.[13]

In addition, to the supervision carried out at the central level, the SBV performs supervision in each of its 62 municipal and provincial branches. The organisation of supervision belongs to municipal and provincial branches, but the chief of banking supervision directs it. Duties of supervision units are to inspect activities of branches of local credit institutions. The current number of staff in the banking supervision department is 200, of whom 100 are assigned to the central office while 100 are supervisors at the municipal and provincial branches. Again, the 1998 Law on the State Bank brought about considerable changes in the organisation of supervision – changes that are summarised in Table 4.4.

In the past SBV supervision has been subject to criticism. Most notably the World Bank (1995) characterised the on-site inspection performed by the SBV as 'one that is largely bottom-up at the branch or sub-branch level, and with a focus on verifying the accuracy of financial statements'. Moreover, the World Bank (1995) notes that 'the work performed during this period (i.e. up till about 1995) was more in the nature of an internal audit, rather than examination'. Since then a number of measures have, however, been undertaken to strengthen banking supervision. First, the powers and responsibilities of the supervisors are (as described in Tables

Table 4.3: SBV supervision before and after the Law on the State Bank – I

	Law on the State Bank	Prior to the law
Legal position	Banking supervision is defined as the professional inspection of the banking sector. Banking supervision is a unit of the state inspectorate at the state bank.	Banking supervision was a unit of the state inspectorate at the state bank.
Functions	Professional supervision and general inspection.	General inspection.
Purpose	To secure the safety of the system of credit institutions. To protect legitimate rights and interests of depositors. To support the implementation of the national monetary policy.	Unclear purpose.
Objects	Organisations and operations of credit institutions. Organisations of operations of non-banking financial institutions. Implementation of regulation on monetary and banking issues of institutions and individuals.	Organisations and operations of credit institutions. Organisations and operations of institutions belonging directly to the State Bank.
Principle	Banking supervision only abides by the law to insure accuracy, objectiveness, transparency, democracy and timing. Banking supervision must not suffer interference from other authorities.	The principles on inspection were stipulated in the ordinance on inspection in general.

Source: Tou (2001)

Table 4.4: SBV supervision before and after the law on the State Bank – II

	Law on the State Bank	Prior to the law
Authority	Central banking supervision of the SBV and banking supervision of municipal and provincial branches. Instructions and assignments between central, municipal and provincial banking supervision are systematic.	Central banking supervision of the SBV and banking supervision of municipal and provincial branches. A vertical system of banking supervision was not clear.
Leadership	Chief and assistant chiefs involved in the central banking supervision. Chief and assistant chiefs at municipal and provincial branches.	Chief and assistant chiefs involved in the central banking supervision. Chief and assistant chiefs at municipal and provincial branches.
Duties	Implementing banking supervision. Implementing functions of a unit of state inspection.	Duties were not made clear.
Powers	The SBV can decide upon, recommend and carry out the penalisation of administrative violations. In addition, the SBV was given the right to make proposals for new ordinances and legislation and the powers to perform inspections. In addition, if the SBV disagrees with government decisions, an official note of the SBV position will be kept in the official records. The chiefs of banking supervision at the central level and the municipal and provincial branches were given the power to suspend the implementation of illegal re-	The SBV could decide upon and recommend but not carry out the penalisation of administrative violations. Other powers were not clear.

Table 4.4: SBV supervision before and after the law on the State Bank – II

	gulations, to suspend the implementation of punishment, and to warn and suspend individuals who hamper inspection.	
Supervisor standards	A supervisor at level 1 was required to have at least three-years of experience in the banking sector.	Unclear regulation.
Relationship with related agencies.	Clear regulation on the relationship between banking supervision and state inspection, the inspection of other agencies and the legislative system was established.	No regulation or guidelines.

Source: Tou (2001)

4.3 and 4.4) stipulated more clearly now. In addition, supervision methodology and settlement has been changed. Banking supervision activities are increasingly focusing on assessing and examining the indices of banking activities instead of checking the bank accounts, books and invoices. In addition, distant supervision activities have been improved.

Still, Vietnamese banking supervision activities do not meet the requirements of global standards. First, notice should be taken of the fact that the SBV supervision department also handles the judgment and treatment of supervision-related complaints. In addition to the potential conflict of interest involved with having an operative institution handling complaints about its own conduct, this model of organisation has also caused difficulties with respect to time and focus. Banking supervisors often spend their hours handling complaints rather than inspecting specific banking issues.

Second, there is a lack of transparency and of equal treatment among state commercial banks, joint-stock commercial banks and branches of foreign banks. This applies to both the inspection results and the post-inspection settlements. Third, the banking supervision system has not yet found a means to properly assess asset quality and risk (World Bank 2002).

Fourth, the inspection process for banking supervisors in Vietnam is weak and still not at an international standard. There is a pronounced weakness *vis-à-vis* systematic collection and analysis of data. In addition, the inspections performed still appear to be based on rules rather than supervisors evaluating a bank's credit policy and asset quality. Finally, international methods and systems like CAMEL[14] have not been implemented in the SOCBs (World Bank 2002) suggesting that supervision is not even across the different types of financial sector institutions.

One reason why the SBV banking supervisors fail to act in line with international standards is the lack of power and competence to change bank accountancy standards to correspond more closely to international standards. In Vietnam bank accounting systems are determined by the overall accountancy standards stipulated by the Ministry of Finance. As a result, it would be difficult for the SBV to formulate a bank accounting system that differs markedly from the Vietnamese accounting system. The process of changing the overall accounting principles to correspond to international standards has been initiated and is currently under implementation. Progress is, however, very slow. This is in part because a process of nature takes time as it involves the formulation of a chart of accounts, the development of an entirely new accounting methodology and the training of staff. The observed delays could, however, also be because a shift to international accounting and auditing practices could reveal that problems of non-performing loans and weak balance sheets are larger than current official estimates.

According to Cohen (2003), a running dispute over the adoption of international auditing practices in the management of central bank accounts and reserves has caused the IMF to effectively suspend its programme with the SBV. The IMF board is reluctant to lend more money to Vietnam before it has assurances that the SBV can adopt and manage international auditing practices of its central bank accounts and reserves. The SBV, however, maintains that it has never signed up for independent audits that run counter to prevailing laws – bringing the dispute with the IMF to a stalemate.

In conclusion, one can identify a number of both direct and indirect measures that if implemented could improve the quality, and timeliness of SBV supervision. A central question, which, however, remains to be addressed, is whether the SBV should continue to perform and be responsible for banking supervision in Vietnam. This is, as stated previously, essentially a political decision. One can nevertheless identify the following potential benefits from such a separation. First, the separation of the supervisory division from the SBV would serve to increase the distance between the SBV and its former operative functions (the current SOCBs), which in turn would be likely to minimise the risk of preferential treatment and/ or outsider attempts to bias SBV policies and rulings. Second, the remaining narrower set of SBV objectives could make the quest for increased SBV independence (see above) easier and more feasible. Less conflict of interest would occur and efforts could be more concentrated. Third, any conflicts of interest between the overall monetary policies and the supervision of the banking sector would be made more transparent and would have to be settled through discussion and negotiation between the two institutions (i.e. the SBV and a new independent bank supervision institution). This could, for example, be a situation where the bank supervision institution in order to better deal with overdue debt in the banking sector would prefer a more expansive monetary policy.

On the other hand, one should not neglect the operational, political and legal obstacles, facing the creation of a new and independent supervisory institution. These range from the costs incurred to the political power struggles that might occur between new and old state institutions. A complete evaluation of supervisory practices of the State Bank of Vietnam (SBV) is planned for the future. The study has yet to begin, but the implementation of the recommendations from this evaluation is to be completed before the end of 2005. One of the issues that will be considered during this process is the establishment of an independent control and audit institution, reporting directly to the Audit Committee of the Board of Directors. In addition, talks have indicated that a completion of the guidelines for how to resolve/intervene in troubled banks will take place. The analysis presented here suggests that the SBV and the Vietnamese government in this process should at least consider the pros and cons of a complete separation of supervisory duties from the SBV.

NPLS AND AMCS

The reasons for focusing on the problem of non-performing loans are legion. First, resolving the NPL problem remains a key obstacle to the transformation of the banking sector since the NPLs prevent banks from becoming profitable and taking in new lending. Second, the SBV plays a key role in the measures taken to address the NPL problem, and third, because very little information about this process is currently publicly available (see Chapter 1).

As already mentioned in Chapter 2, the SOCBs granted the majority of NPLs, many dating years back, to state-owned enterprises in difficulty or under the direction of the government, to achieve social or economic objectives. The close ties between the government and the SOE sector mean that the approach taken to solve the NPL problem is an important indicator of the overall political will to reform. In other words, does the government have the necessary resolve and needed political will to address problems that predominantly result from past policy shortcomings?

The problem of NPLs could, however, extend beyond the financial sector. No information is currently available about the magnitude and distribution of inter-corporate debts between SOEs, nor is it known how these relate to bank debts. In addition, the World Bank (2002b) reports that anecdotal evidence indicates that some SOEs have been on-lending credit obtained from SOCBs to private-sector small and medium-sized enterprises. Experience from other former centrally planned economies indicates that inter-corporate debts can be sizeable. This could substantially complicate efforts to restructure SOEs and state-owned banks as it raises difficult questions of priority and relative importance between SOE obligations to other SOEs versus the obligations towards the SOCBs.

Regardless of whether or not inter-corporate debt of any magnitude exists, holding a large fraction of NPLs is almost certain to have had detrimental effects on banking sector performance. The general channels through which NPLs can exert a negative influence on banking performance include: (i) the diversion of managerial time and skills from other banking activities, (ii) the reduction in funds available for new loans. The latter constraint arises in part because prudential ratios stipulated by bank legislation restrict the amount of credit available for new loans and in part because funds are used to roll-over and/or ever-green the non-performing loans and (iii) the loss of depositor and inter-bank confidence in the banking sector reduces incentives to channel savings or investments to the banks.

In addition to taxing banking sector resources, NPLs may also have an adverse effect on bank lending behaviour by making banks averse to risk, which in turn could affect bank behaviour. Diamond (1991) has shown that short-term credit represents an important channel of bank control over borrowers on markets characterised by high risk and information problems. The idea is that by offering short-term credit the bank effectively puts a limit on the time an opportunistic borrower can exploit its creditors without being in default. If correct, the problems of asymmetric information and forced exposure to high risk SOE borrowers can help explain the shortage of long-term credit in Vietnam. A higher level of risk can, however, also induce a bank to take on even riskier loans (to gamble for re-surrection). If practised by the majority of the banks, this could result in a credit crunch that in turn would increase the probability of a systemic crisis coupled with further loss of investor and depositor confidence in the sector.

The initial Vietnamese response to a growing recognition that the presence of NPLs was likely to impede bank performance was one of regulatory forbearance. It was essentially hoped that high levels of economic growth and the ongoing efforts to improve banking sector performance would cause the NPL problems to be resolved without significant financial commitments and/or direct involvement by the government. However, as the necessary improvements in both macroeconomic performance and bank management were slow to appear in the years following the East Asian Crisis, it became increasingly clear that following a strategy of regulatory forbearance would not solve the NPL problem. Hence, to clean up the SOCB balance sheets and address the NPL problem, it was decided to introduce a new type of institution in Vietnam, the asset management company (AMC). Using AMCs has to some extent become the standard international response to NPL problems in financial sectors and AMCs have been established in a large number of countries, including most of the neighbouring East Asian countries following the EAFC.

As mentioned in Chapter 2, the problems associated with banks' balance sheets being burdened by a large share of NPLs are not unique to Vietnam. Indeed, following the EAFC all countries that had been directly affected by the crisis were burdened with a large volume of non-performing assets, including non-performing or past due loans and real estate and other assets pledged as collateral for loans. Based on the official statistics depicted in Table 4.5, it would moreover appear that the NPL problems were even larger in the other countries of the region. As is the case in Vietnam, several of the depicted countries are thought to have employed a definition of NPLs, which is more lenient than recommended by international standards.

As a response to this problem the East Asian countries all chose to set up a system of AMCs. In general terms, an AMC is an institution established to acquire, manage and recover non-performing assets of troubled or failed financial institutions. Following Cooke and Foley (2000), it is possible to identify three different institutional set-ups that can be used when introducing AMCs in a financial sector: (i) a centralised state-owned AMC; (ii) decentralised AMCs operating as separate departments within each bank; and (iii) decentralised AMCs operating as separate legal entities addressing the particular problems of a troubled bank.

It is important to point out that no blueprint exists regarding which of the three types of AMC set-ups to employ to a given set of circumstances. Cooke and Foley (2000) suggest that a centralised AMC has advantages when the NPL problem is of a systemic magnitude and/or when special legal powers and specifically tailored legislation are needed to override the judicial branch. In addition, choosing a central AMC is more likely to be effective if the human capital and specialist skills necessary to operate AMCs are in limited supply

Table 4.5: NPLs in East Asia in 1998

	NPLs in peak year of crisis	Estimated amount of government debt to pay for bank restructuring	Annual interest cost of government debt to pay for bank restructuring
	Share of loans (%)	Share of GDP (%)	Share of GDP (%)
Thailand	50	70	32
Indonesia	70	53	29
Malaysia	30	42	18
Korea	35	35	18
Philippines	15	5	4

Source: Cooke and Foley (2000)

in the financial sector. As can be seen from Table 4.6 most countries in the region eventually chose to introduce a centralised AMC.

According to Rajan and Bird (2001) all of the East Asian economies have made 'some headway in reducing NPLs'. In Korea and Malaysia the combined effect of the economic recovery and the AMC effort have caused a reduction in NPL ratios for commercial banks to less than 10 per cent.[15] In contrast, NPLs have remained high in Thailand (about 30 per cent). Rajan and Bird cautiously attribute the lack of success in Thailand to the Thai government's preference for a market-based approach to financial restructuring. Cooke and Foley (2000) moreover note that the decentralised approach chosen in Thailand was not without problems. To be more specific, the bank-based AMCs did not appear to be guiding and coordinating their efforts to resolve the country's NPL problems. Still plagued by a high level of non-performing loans, the Thai government in February 2001 finally decided to establish a centralised AMC with broad special powers to resolve the critical situation of the banking sector.

In Indonesia, the central AMC is estimated to control approximately 75 per cent of total NPLs, but the combination of powerful, unco-operative borrowers and an inadequate legislative framework continue to hamper the subsequent recovery and restructuring of assets.

Table 4.6: AMC set-up in East Asian countries

	Model	Chosen Approach
Thailand	Initially both central and decentralised.	Financial Sector Restructuring Authority (FRA) evaluates finance companies' rehabilitation plans and sells their assets.
	Subsequently a central model was chosen	An asset management company acts as bidder of last resort for FRA's bad assets. Radhanasin Bank* acts as bidder for FRA's good assets. Bank-based asset management companies work out NPLs for commercial banks (both private and state).
Indonesia	Decentralised	Indonesian Bank Restructuring Agency supervises banks in need of restructuring and manages assets acquired in the bank restructuring process.
Malaysia	Central	Special purpose vehicle for the management and disposition of banking system NPLs.
Korea	Central	Special purpose vehicle for the management and disposition of banking system non-performing assets.

Note: The Radhanasin Bank (RAB) was initially created to manage quality assets of the failed finance companies, leaving the bad assets to the AMC. In January 1998, however, the government announced that the RAB would no longer serve in this capacity but instead act as a commercial bank
Source: Cooke and Foley (2000)

Regardless of whether a centralised or decentralised approach is chosen, Cooke and Foley identify a number of key lessons to emerge from the experience of other East Asian countries. First, addressing the NPL problem is *not* equivalent to addressing the factors responsible for creating the problem in the first place. Failure to address the causes of the NPL problems is to invite a repetition. A realistic assessment of the cause, size and character of the problem is a key starting point for any attempt to address the NPL problems.

Second, the government must assess the legal infrastructure prior to establishing the AMC. This implies ensuring that the legal system and legal powers are in place to permit an effective and swift case management and that bankruptcy, tax, property ownership, collateral and foreclosure laws are both adequate and reflected in court rulings. If the legal infrastructure appears inadequate, measures must be taken to provide the AMCs with the necessary special legal powers and/or legislation.

Third, the use of AMCs and the issue of resolving NPLs is a complex matter, and the government should consider establishing an independent supervisory board responsible for a balanced, non-partisan oversight of the efforts and results. The board should have both industry and government representatives. It should *not* be directly involved in the daily operations.

Finally, Cook and Foley (2000) note that the complexity involved in establishing and operating an AMC requires that the government should make sure that policies and institutions are developed to promote openness and transparency in the process. Lack of transparency can result in a conflict of interest, or the appearance thereof, which can diminish public confidence in the integrity of the process.

Several aspects of the NPL problem and the financial sector in Vietnam appear to fit the circumstances under which one would suggest the introduction of a centralised AMC.[16] These include:

- The deficiencies in key national legal and judicial frameworks such as those concerning collateral, land ownership, transfer of loans and creditor rights, and land usage rights. In addition, the majority of the loans made to SOEs were made without collateral, making it very difficult to claim assets to recover the loan.

- The need to coordinate NPL assessment and restructuring with ongoing SOE reforms. This includes tackling potentially powerful and politically connected debtors, who might oppose the process and/or seek to take advantage of the situation and the relatively ineffective legal recourse.

- The potential benefits from establishing linkages to the ongoing efforts to reform and restructure SOCBs. A centralised AMC would provide the government with an opportunity to accelerate and guide bank restructuring through the conditions it attaches to the purchase of NPLs.

- The scarcity of managerial and analytical talent in the sector. A single entity would be in a better position to reap economies of scale and make the best use of the human capital available.

- The thin or non-existing secondary markets for financial assets make it difficult for separate AMCs to obtain uniform and transparent valuations and conditions of sale. In addition, AMC experience in other ASEAN countries has been marred by a lack of interested buyers. A centralised AMC with a more direct government involvement would be in a better position to legitimise the bundling of NPLs and/or to offer discounts, if a lack of interested buyers also turns out to be a problem in Vietnam.

Following the decision to use AMCs, the State Bank of Vietnam initially suggested that Vietnam should introduce a central nationwide AMC. A range of political, legal and technical hurdles, however, hampered the implementation of this first choice. Instead it was decided to opt for a decentralised approach, such that each SOCB would have its own AMC. The extent to which the decision to introduce decentralised AMCs went against the wishes of the SBV is difficult to gauge. It is, however, tempting to link the fact that the initial (and by all counts sound) recommendation made by the SBV was disregarded to the aforementioned lack of SBV autonomy.

To implement the decision, the prime minister initially published an Official Letter in February 2000, allowing state commercial banks to establish companies for debt management and exploitation of mortgaged assets on the basis of an approved plan for the settlement of commercial bank NPLs. This plan was, however, superseded in October 2001 when the prime minister promulgated a new decision establishing a company for debt management and asset exploitation under commercial banks. The new decision, using a higher-ranked legislative instrument, has wider applications than the earlier Official Letter. All types of security were now covered by the regulation instead of only mortgaged assets. The importance of the extension to include non-collateralised loans rests on the fact that most NPLs to SOEs were given without collateral. The structure of the AMC system in Vietnam is illustrated in Figure 4.1.

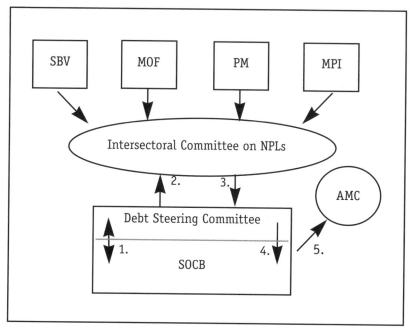

Figure 4.1: The structure of the Vietnamese AMC system

The procedure for each SOCB is as follows: within each SOCB a specially set up Debt Steering Committee works with SOCB staff on the basis of diagnostic audits to identify the NPLs. The NPLs identified by the Debt Steering Committee are subsequently submitted for approval to the Intersectoral Committee on NPL which consists of representatives from the State Bank of Vietnam (SBV), the Ministry of Finance (MOF), the Prime Minister's Office (PM) and the Ministry of Planning and Investment (MPI). This committee considers the proposal submitted by the Debt Steering Committee and then communicates their decision back to the Debt Steering Committee who subsequently tells the SOCB which loans should be transferred to its AMC. Similar processes are carried out in the other three SOCBs.

Although detailed plans on how the AMCs are to operate are currently not publicly available, some details of the original restructuring plan for the Vietcombank (VCB) completed during the fall of 2001 have been made public.[17] The performance criteria for the VCB at the end of the three-year reform period included a capital–assets ratio of 6 to 8 per cent, a return on assets of at least 0.5 per cent and NPLs below 4 per cent of total loans outstanding. As for the NPLs in the VCB, the plan was to complete the loan classification and recovery plans for loans to the 50 largest debtors of the VCB before the end of 2001. Recovery plans for the remaining loans were subsequently to be worked out before the end of 2002. The recovery rate for the LWU associated with the VCB was tentatively scheduled to gradually increase from 10 per cent in 2001, rising to 25 per cent in 2002, and 35 per cent in 2003.

In addition, the Vietnamese Bank for Investment and Development (VBID) announced in January 2002 that it had set up its own AMC. Some details of the organisation and objectives of this company were also made public: the AMC responsible for the VBID had an initial chartered capital of 30 billion dong, and will inherit all VBID outstanding debts (secured and unsecured) as well as the assets pledged for such debts. It was hoped that the AMC would secure at least 40 billion dong in bad debts.[18] In addition, the AMC of the VBID was authorised to sell assets mortgaged with the VBID at market prices to the public through the State Auction Centre, or to other AMCs. The AMC of the VBID was also given powers to restructure outstanding debts by rescheduling, cutting interest rates and transferring debts into investment.

As for debt restructuring in private banks, two government decisions indicate that it would like to facilitate and speed up debt restructuring in the private sector: the decision in October 2001 allowed commercial banks to set up their own AMCs, and in a directive dated 7 January 2002, the State Bank governor gave commercial banks greater autonomy in handling overdue debts.

The massive growth in bank credit has, as noted in Chapter 2, reduced the ratio of NPLs to total loans through an increase in the denominator. The AMCs have, however, also made some progress in resolving loans. The AMCs and the SOCBs have thus been able to resolve approximately one-third of the originally estimated 23 billion dong of NPLs (see Chapter 2). These were mainly collateralised loans – i.e. presumably mainly consisting of loans to private companies. What remains is therefore most likely the difficult task of resolving the uncollateralised loans made predominantly to SOEs.

Given the limited and fragmented information about the nature and extent of the NPL problem and the specific conditions under which the AMCs will operate any predictions of future performance and success rate is difficult. One can, however, point to three key issues that are likely to be of central importance to the efforts to resolve the NPL problem. The three issues, which will be discussed in turn below, are: (i) the autonomy and legal power of the decentralised AMCs; (ii) the initial assessment and understanding of the problem; and (iii) the recruitment and training of skilled personnel.

Turning first to the issue of the autonomy and legal power of the decentralised AMCs, it is evident that the extent to which a decentralised approach can still be successful depends upon: (i) how much the government is willing to empower the AMCs *vis-à-vis* the judicial system; and (ii) the supporting policies and institutions established by the central government and the SBV.

As for judicial empowerment, it could, for example, consider attributing special powers to the asset management company. These include powers relating to the transfer of loans and collateral and their enforcement as well as procedures relating to registration and transfer of title documents evidencing ownership. A difficult trade-off, however, exists between ensuring that the decentralised AMCs have the necessary power to operate and minimising the degree of special powers granted to non-legal units. In some countries AMCs have been given powers that exceed what is normally advisable. In Malaysia, for example, the government provided its AMC with extensive authority to circumvent existing bankruptcy laws. In the US following the savings and loans scandal, the Resolution Trust Corporation was authorised to override state laws and set aside burdensome contracts. Adequate controls need to be in place to ensure that such powers are not misused.

As for the above-mentioned supporting institutions that could possibly facilitate the operations of the decentralised AMCs, they could include an overall supervisory institution with the objective of ensuring homogeneous valuations. Experience from Thailand indicates that such institutions help ensure that homogenous NPLs are valued alike across SOCBs and that fire sales of low-quality assets are avoided. It is not known whether the Intersectoral Committee for NPLs merely considers the NPLs for political approval or whether they undertake a coordinating role across the four SOCBs.

Finally, operational funding for start-up and operations for the individual AMC should be supplied from a non-partisan source – i.e. not from the bank whose NPLs the AMC is attempting to resolve. As is evident from Table 4.7, AMCs in other East Asian countries receive their operational funding from a multitude of different sources, including asset recoveries, issuance of equity, bond programmes and the government.

Next, turning to the importance of an initial realistic assessment of the size and character of the problem, the ADB study mentioned above furthermore points to the fact that addressing the NPL problem does not necessarily imply addressing the factors responsible for creating the problem in the first place.

The groundwork prior to establishing the AMCs therefore constitutes a real test of the governments will and ability to undertake in-depth reforms of the financial sector. Will the restructuring and re-capitalisation of the four major SOCBs imply a change in lending practices? So far the evidence presented in Chapter 2 appears to be negative in the case of Vietnam. This applies both to the continuation of policy lending and the fact that the massive increase in SOCB lending during the period 2000–02 does not appear to have been based on proper risk assessments of the borrowers and their projects.

Table 4.7: Operational funding for AMCs in East Asia

Thailand	Indonesia	Malaysia	Korea	Philippines
Government supplied seed capital. The AMC has the ability to issue bonds to purchase assets. Finally, the AMC can issue promissory notes to cover interest expenses	Asset recovery and sale of equity will cover some. Government guaranteed bonds replace acquired NPLs. In return, the state receives equity in the banks.	75% of funding will originate from the AMC Bond Programme. The remainder is funded by loans from the government and SOEs.	90% of funding stems from bonds issued by the AMC. The remaining 10% originate from the Central Bank.	Funding is provided by the Department of Finance.

Source: Cooke and Foley (2000)

Finally, obtaining and maintaining the necessary managerial and analytical talent is an often-overlooked dimension of institutional change. Given the fact that the Vietnamese government has established several highly specialised and complex financial institutions in a country where skilled manpower is already in short supply, the approach taken to overcome this problem will be of central importance in achieving government goals.

AMC staff will require expertise in asset management, including asset appraisal, property management and conducting workouts. In addition, experience in banking, legal matters, accounting, marketing and public relations will also be required. In the short run, the government can perhaps obtain such skills and through foreign specialists conducting capacity building courses. It is, however, a short-term gap-filling approach that cannot substitute for extensive investments in enhancing the capacity of the domestic institutions responsible for the training of financial sector specialists

CONCLUDING REMARKS

This chapter has provided an analysis of some of the key areas related to the reforms of the SBV. Overall, it must be concluded that the SBV with its current capacity cannot effectively develop and execute national monetary policies, and that the SBV remains operationally and politically dependent upon support from other government agencies. The Vietnamese tradition of consensus governance appears to be in direct conflict with the conventional emphasis on creating autonomous central banks. This is likely to be the case almost regardless of whether the direct (legislative) approach or the indirect (lobby building) approach is followed, although the expected increased presence of foreign banks is likely to increase the indirect pressure in the coming years.

In terms of the SBV role as a facilitator and organiser of financial markets, the second section of the chapter briefly considered the current status of the market for government bonds and the interbank market for domestic and foreign currency. Both the market for government bonds and the market for foreign currency appear to lack depth and breadth, reflecting in part their early stage of development. The government appears to have paid little attention to facilitating the development of a market-based benchmark yield curve, and a number of legislative restrictions restrict the growth of the secondary market for treasury bills. Conducting monetary policies through open market operations consequently seems to be too ambitious at the moment.

As for the role of the SBV as a supervisor and regulator of the financial markets and institutions, progress can be noted, although it is just as clear that there is still a long way to go. This is particularly the case with reference to adopting the international accounting and auditing practices that are likely to improve the overall transparency of the sector. In this context, the creation of a separate institution that is responsible for supervision and regulation could have the potential for further improvements in this area.

Finally, addressing the problem of NPLs and the use of a new type of institution, namely asset management companies (AMCs), a number of problems related to judiciary, administrative and human-capital-related constraints were identified in relation to the use of decentralised AMCs in Vietnam. The limited autonomy and legal power of the decentralised AMCs, in combination with the noted persistence of policy lending and a low stock of human capital, consequently makes it highly unlikely that the recent progress in resolving NPLs can continue in the future.

NOTES

1   See Eijffinger and de Haan (1996), for a review of these studies.

2   One could also include an assessment of the degree of financial independence of the SBV among the *internal* factors potentially curbing overall operational independence. Following Beckerman (1997), the financial independence of a central bank is defined as the requisite quantity and composition of capital to make the central bank able to perform a credible and effective macroeconomic management of money and credit.

3   As already mentioned in Chapter 2, most analysts regarded the 1998 Law of the State Bank as a setback compared to the autonomy bestowed upon the SBV prior to the passing of the law. As noted by Klump and Gottwald (2003), Murray (1999) represents an exception to the rule.

4   Whether or not the lack of automatic rules of action can be attributed to the Vietnamese tradition of consensus governance cannot be said with certainty, but it *is* clear that such rules and their expected consequences would circumvent the normal consensus-orientated decision-making processes in Vietnam.

5   Note: most chiefs of banking supervision are officials from the state bank and none are officials from the Ministry of Finance or a state-owned enterprise.

6   Some of the provincial offices have a staff of over a hundred people.

7   The term 'bonds' is used in the broadest sense and includes all tradable fixed-income instruments such as bills (usually with a maturity of less than one year), notes (with maturities between one and five years) and bonds (most often with maturities of more than five years).

8   As pointed out by Herring and Chatusripitak (2000) government bonds are traditionally treated as if they were risk free although some risk of course will always remain. What is needed is not a complete risk free asset, but that the assets that are used to form a benchmark

share the same risk of default over the entire term structure. This is normally assumed to be the case with governments.

9   Relying on foreign banks or even issuing corporate debt outside the country is also a possibility. The increased exposure to foreign exchange risk, high transaction costs, asymmetric information and in some cases domestic legislation, however, prevent this from being an option in most developing countries.

10   Hong Kong provides one example of how authorities developed a benchmark yield curve despite running fiscal surpluses. Here, the proceeds accruing to the government through the issues of Hong Kong dollar bills and notes were subsequently invested in international markets.

11   Note that preventing this from happening is a very important consideration in the process of deciding the size of the bond issue. However, lack of previous experience with Vietnamese bonds on the international market and the fact that other priorities also influence the design of the bond makes this difficult.

12   The implicit assumption is, of course, that staff will be expanded to take care of supervision tasks but that the capacity of the central governor remains unchanged.

13   The fact that the treatment of complaints over SBV supervision is handled by a division within the SBV and not a separate unit outside the SBV is addressed below.

14   CAMEL is an acronym denoting the use of an internationally recognised framework for assessing the Capital adequacy, Asset quality, Management, Earnings and Liquidity of banks. Recently, an 'S' for Sensitivity to market risk was added, making the acronym CAMELS. The system is intended to provide an overall rating of a bank's condition at the end of an on-site bank examination. The rating is made available to bank management and supervisory personnel only.

15   This is also noted by Park and Lee (2002), who single out Korea as having been more aggressive and effective in restructuring its financial sector.

16   Lan (2000) also suggests that a centralised AMC would be more suitable in Vietnam.

17   As pointed out by Cohen (2003), the Vietcombank represents an important point of reference not only for the SOCBs but for all banks in Vietnam. This is in part due to better past performance and in part because the Vietcombank has been selected as the Vietnamese

counterpart in a twinning arrangement with a consortium led by the Dutch ING Group. If successful, this twinning arrangement will result in a complete overhaul of all aspects of the VCB, ranging from credit risk management and internal audits to financial restructuring and product diversification.

18   To compare, by the end of 2001, the VBID had total outstanding debts of 42,500 billion dong.

CHAPTER 5

Financial services for the agricultural sector

The purpose of this chapter is to give a brief description of how banks operate in the agricultural sector. This includes both the specific problems encountered by the different types of banks and their interrelation in the market. The choice of the agricultural sector for this case study rests upon the fact that this financial sector is the largest and most important sector in terms of both employment and value of output.

The most important formal financial institution serving the rural areas is the Vietnamese Bank for Agriculture and Rural Development (the VBARD). Given its importance to the agricultural sector, the VBARD is considered separately below. Subsequently, the analysis moves on to consider a number of problems related to the tension created between the rapid increase in financial sector outreach, on the one hand, and the historical legacy of a policy directed and tightly controlled monobank system on the other. This has resulted in a number of structural problems that urgently need to be addressed if the positive development in the agricultural sector is to continue. The three problems that will be considered in more detail in this chapter are: (i) the lack of competition between financial institutions in effect serving separated segments of the rural population; (ii) the regulated and in some cases heavily subsidized interest rates, which among other things stifle financial innovation and restrict the formal institutions from obtaining sustainability; and (iii) the limited mobilisation of savings that restricts the resource base and the outreach of the financial sector.

The initiation of the Doi Moi reforms, and in particular the land laws adopted in 1988, have led to a radical transformation of the

Vietnamese agricultural sector.[1] The acceptance of the private family farm as the principal unit of agricultural production and the gradual introduction of rural non-farm enterprises resulted in a rapid and sustained increase in agricultural production for both domestic and export markets (the latter consisting mainly of rice, coffee, pepper and cashews). The drive to obtain and expand the full potential of the agricultural sector has in turn increased the pressure to establish a viable, market-based financial system for the rural farms and enterprises.

The increased demand for financial services for the rural areas quickly led to the establishment of new, specialised institutions predominantly directed towards servicing rural populations. First, there was the credit cooperative system that, however, collapsed in 1990 (see Chapter 1) that was subsequently followed by government-established institutions such as the Vietnamese Bank for Agriculture and Rural Development (VBARD) founded in 1990, the gradual establishment of People's Credit Funds (PCFs) from 1993 and onwards and the Vietnamese Bank for the Poor (VBP) established in 1996. The government also increased pressure on existing banks and mass organisations to increase their outreach in rural areas. As a consequence, the share of rural households having access to credit jumped from 9 per cent in 1992 to 30 per cent in 1994.

At the time of writing the estimate is that about 60 per cent of rural households have access to formal and semi-formal financial services[2] – an impressive increase in outreach in just little over a decade. The segments of rural populations who are still not served or underprovided with financial services include the ultra poor, people in remote areas[3] and people who are not members of a mass organisation.

The VBARD was established on 26 March 1988 under the Law on Credit Institutions, and it has subsequently played a major role in the provision of investment capital to agriculture and rural areas. In terms of customers, the VBARD is the largest bank in Vietnam. In 2001, bank customers included 6,000 enterprises and 7.5 million business households. The VBARD also has the densest network of branch offices in Vietnam and a staff of more than 24,000. Total credit in 2001 was 60,054 billion dong, of which medium and long-term credit accounted for almost 43 per cent or 25,684 billion dong. Looking more closely at the distribution of VBARD credit in 2000, it can be seen that 37,818 billion dong, or 63 per cent, was given to households in rural sectors, 21 per cent or 12,614 billion dong went to SOEs, while privately owed enterprises received 3,211 billion dong amounting to 5.3 per cent of total credit. Only 92 billion dong or 0.15 per cent of total credit went to the collective sector. A survey of a number of agricultural cooperatives indicated that the majority of those surveyed faced difficulties accessing credit from the VBARD because they lacked the assets required. In fact, many heads of cooperatives had to use their own assets as collateral to borrow capital for the cooperatives.

Classifying the lenders by their principal economic activity, the credit provided by VBARD was allocated as shown in Figure 5.1.

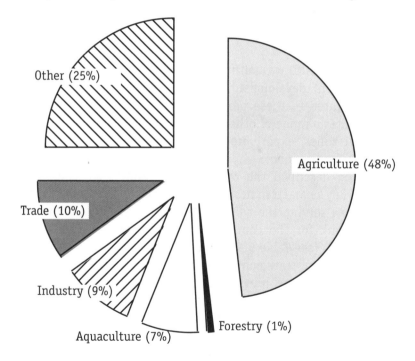

Figure 5.1: VBARD allocation of credit in 2000

In addition, the VBARD was required to carry out a number of national policy credit programmes. By the end of 2001, the results of implementing these were:

- Credit for the project on upgrading houses built on stilts in flooded areas: 930 billion dong (share of outstanding debts collected: 44 per cent);

- Credit for the project on reducing adverse impacts of storm No. 5 in 1997: 841 billion dong (share of outstanding debts collected: 27 per cent);

- Credit for the project on reducing adverse impacts of drought in 1998: 41 billion dong (share of outstanding debts collected: 40 per cent);

- Credit for the project on reducing adverse impacts of floods in 1999: 135 billion dong (share of outstanding debts collected: 42 per cent).

Finally, the VBARD was authorized to allocate capital to a number of government development projects. At the end of 2001, total capital granted to these projects was 843.9 billion dong. VBARD also operates a range of other financial services such as lending to industrial zones, export processing zones, co-sponsored lending, guarantee and leasing.[4]

Having described the operations of VBARD we can turn to compare key characteristics of the three most dominant financial institutions serving the agricultural sector: the VBARD, the Vietnamese Bank for the Poor (VBP) and the People's Credit Funds System (PCF) (see Table 5.1).

The mission statements and the mode of operation of the reviewed institutions provide an explanation for the lack of competition between the rural financial institutions. Exercising significant direct control over all three institutions, the government has laid down an explicit division of labour towards providing financial services for all income segments of the rural population.

In addition, the local communes, people's committees and mass organisations play a crucial role in the identification, screening

Table 5.1: Key characteristics of financial institutions in the agricultural sector

	VBARD	VBP	PCF
Year of establish ment	1988 as a depart- ment of former monobank. Be- came operational in December 1990.	Established in 1995 as a state- owned, non- profit bank.	The Rural Finance Project began in March 1994.
Mission state- ment	The explicit focus of VBARD is on financing all types of enter- prises in rural areas.	The explicit in- tention is to eli- minate hunger and alleviate poverty through the provision of small loans to poor households.	The objective is to supplant the failed credit cooperatives and to restore con- fidence in the for- mal financial sector.
No. of clients	Above 4 million.	About 2.2 million.	Approximately 0.7 million.
Customer profile	About 90% of all formal credit to rural households was handled by the VBARD in 1997, although this share might include some handled by the VBP.	Only people classified as poor are eligible for loans. Monthly income is con- verted into rice value. Cut off values are: urban areas less than 25 kg per person, rural areas under 20 kg and in mountainous areas less than 15 kg.	The following is known about the composition of members of PCFs: 66% are farmers, 20% are rural traders and 11% are rural artisans and small entre- preneurs. 15 founding mem- bers of a LCF have to buy shares amounting to 3,333 million dong per person that can be paid in instal- ments over a num- ber of years. Rank- and-file members

Table 5.1: Key characteristics of financial institutions in the agricultural sector

	VBARD	VBP	PCF
			have to buy a qualification share amounting to 50,000 dong.
Number of branch offices	At the end of 1996 the VBARD had 2,564 branch offices. In addition, mobile banking units are operating transaction offices at the commune level. The VBARD is one of the largest networks in Vietnam and the largest provider of credit to the rural sector.	Use infrastructure and staff of the VBARD. VBP also collaborates with other organisations (ministries, mass organisations, etc) for screening, supervision and support for the groups.	In September 1998 there were 988 People's Credit Funds established in 35 of Vietnam's provinces. The total number of members exceeded 600,000 in September 1998.
Portfolio of financial products supplied	Only short- to medium-term credit has been available. Short-term lending accounted for two-thirds of all credit in 2001. Possible collateral is: land-use-rights, real estate and durable consumption goods.	Only one product: a 2–5 year loan without collateral. Interest is payable in monthly instalments but the principal should not be paid before the end of the loan period. In most cases credit is not handed over in cash but in kind.	The loans are small, mainly geared toward production. Only consumer goods are accepted as collateral, not land-use rights.

and follow-up on clients for each type of institution. The result is that the initiative to form joint-liability groups and/or to contact potential lenders comes from the institutions themselves. This is a top-down approach which originates in a desire to divide the market among the institutions in order to extend their outreach. The segments served by the three institutions can be summarised as follows:

- **VBARD**   Until 1995 the primary clientele of the VBARD were the medium and well-to-do farmers, who could provide collateral. Starting from 1995 the VBARD introduced joint-liability groups where small loans are processed via groups. In 1997 about 150,000 joint-liability groups were supported. This initiative has to some extent made VBARD credit available to less well-off households, but the majority of the clients still remain in the upper income segments of the rural population.

- **VBP**   As indicated by its name and the requirement to lend only to people classified as being poor, the VBP serves the less well-off segments. The restriction to supply only one financial product has, however, been found to restrict the ability of the VBP to reach the very poor. These destitute households have frequently been found to regard VBP loans of typically VND 1–2 million as being too large. According to the Asian Development Bank (ADB) (1999), numerous reports exist of poor households actually turning down loan offers. In addition, many poor households oppose the special repayment structure of VBP loans where only interest payments are made until the instalment that includes the entire principal of the loan. Many households, however, are likely to assess that the postponement of the payment of the principal until the end of the loan period represents too high a risk, preferring instead small and frequent instalments of both principal and interest. Another factor contributing to the exclusion of the very poor from the formal financial system is the transactions costs when applying for a loan.

- **PCFs**   The PCFs require borrowers to buy shares in the local credit fund. In addition, screening mechanisms have been built in through the use of local people's committees and the practice of paying out loans in kind. This means that the PCF system predominantly caters for the better off households – in effect excluding poor households who are left with a choice between the VBP and informal finance.

In evaluating the potential negative effects of this lack of competition it is, however, important to point out that financial sector analysts are divided on the question of how important increased financial sector competition is. One group argues that lack of competition will have adverse effects on financial sector performance and development. These include limited financial innovation, lack of incentives to reduce costs and poor quality of services. Another group points to panel data analyses (Demirgüc-Kunt and Detragiache 1998), suggesting that banking sector fragility often increases as a result of the erosion of franchise values that follow from financial sector liberalisation. The key problem is that the countries in question frequently fail to build an appropriate institutional framework for the supervision and regulation of the financial sector. As a result governments find it difficult to curb and control bank behaviour. Banks whose franchise values are eroded shift to riskier business strategies in an attempt to gamble for their resurrection. In many developing countries the end result is costly financial sector crises.

The dispute over whether or not financial sector liberalisation is beneficial has led to the emergence of alternatives and increasing competition. Hence, Hellmann *et al.* (2000) propose an alternative strategy of financial restraint. One basic aspect of their model is that creating profit opportunities for banks will result in banks becoming more stable institutions with better incentives for monitoring borrowers. This in turn will reduce the moral hazard problems when banks imprudently gamble for their survival. As a result overall financial sector stability will improve.

The question of which approach would be suitable for the Vietnamese rural financial sector is not an easy one to answer. The overall lack of transparency in the financial sector (in combination with non-standardised accounting procedures) obstructs attempts to evaluate the frailty of the individual institutions. Interest rates in the institutions serving the rural sector are heavily subsidised and subject to close government control. The provision of subsidised interest rates has for a long time been a point of discussion between the donor community and the government of Vietnam.

The donor community points to international experience with subsidised rural credit programmes in LDCs resulting in massive loan losses, low savings mobilisation and heavy losses to both governments and international donors. In addition, subsidised credit programmes have been found to lead to lacklustre market discipline. They have also had detrimental effects on lending behaviour and managerial competencies and incentives. This has, among other things, led the donor community to refrain from refinancing the VBP.

The government of Vietnam, on the other hand, has maintained subsidised interest rates as part of a policy to ensure equitable growth, redistribution of wealth and poverty alleviation. The government has, however, recently indicated an increased willingness to reconsider existing policies of subsidised interest rates. The following negative effects of operating with subsidised interest rates can be identified:

- **Damaging the perception of credit**. The subsidised low interest rates led to a rush for loans from the VBP and the VBARD. While there is no evidence that subsidised loans saturates the demand for credit, the cheap loans reinforce a common impression that the low interest loans are a right and not a contractual agreement. In addition, the perception that loans at a higher rate are exploitative makes a shift back to market-based rates increasingly difficult.

- **Obstructing the mobilisation of savings**. The cap on lending rates (in combination with the generally high operating costs resulting from expanding outreach in rural areas) implies that lending/deposit spreads are low. As a result, the incentive of savers to channel their funds to the banks weakens as does that of the bank to mobilise savings (if the bank is not making a profit from on-lending deposits due to, for example, the high risks associated with borrower projects, why bother to go to the trouble of mobilising savings?). In total, fewer funds are mobilised for investments.

- **Lowering the quality of financial services**. Low margins lead to transformation of the credit culture that make it cruder and stripped of additional services. This has a detrimental effect upon the innovative, timely and balanced provision of financial services. In addition, banks seek to shift obligations (preparation and training of customers, pre-screening of loan applicants, collection of borrower payments and client supervision) on to clients or their intermediary structures (mass organisations) in order to save costs. This leads to a less focused development of skills and knowledge within the financial institutions.

On the positive side, it has been pointed out that subsidised interest rates mean that the psychological barrier of poor households toward taking a loan is lowered. This may be true in some cases. Existing evidence indicates that the assumption that the interest rate offered is a crucial factor for sustainable lending to poor households is incorrect. The ADB visited a number of micro finance credit projects in Vietnam. Everywhere staff emphasised that a minimum of guidance and training of the poor was needed in order for them to be able make profitable use of loans. This is a lesson that has emerged from a number of projects directed at providing credit to poor households, including the much publicised and copied Grameen Bank in Bangladesh. As a consequence, one German NGO (Misereor) operating in Vietnam has introduced a special training margin of 0.1 per cent that is built into the interest rate to cover the cost of training and guidance. Affiliated lenders are reportedly quite satisfied with this model. In conclusion, the significance of the reduction of the psychological barrier towards loans in poor households is (at best) doubtful, making the effects of operating with subsidised interest rates likely to be predominantly negative.

Mobilising savings was not a priority area for financial institutions until the late 1980s and subsequent attempts to strengthen the performance in this area have generally been moderately successful, at best. Total domestic savings channelled through the formal system rose from 16 per cent to 23 per cent of GDP in the period from 1993 to 1999. However, this is insufficient *vis-à-vis* the need to extend outreach of financial services to remote and mountainous areas. The same can be said of the possibility of obtaining long-term sustainability. Neither of these aims can be achieved as long as the government is the main source of funding. The general picture of limited success in mobilising savings can be attributed to both supply and demand factors, which are, in some areas, mutually reinforcing.

On the supply side, the historical legacy of negative real interest rates during the monobank era and the collapse of the rural credit cooperatives in 1990–91 (see Chapter 1) suggest that the Vietnamese can be characterised as being deeply suspicious of banks. They prefer to keep money in assets with a high degree of liquidity. This can be illustrated with the 1992–93 Vietnam Living Standards Survey (VLSS) that it was found that only about 7.4 per cent of total savings was deposited in banks, some 44 per cent was invested in gold, another 20 per cent went into real estate and more than 10 per cent was kept in cash.

On the demand side, government financing of the rural financial institutions, in combination with the low interest rate margin dictated by the government, reduces incentives to mobilise savings. However, looking at the performance at the institutional level reveals considerable differences across the major state-controlled institutions. The PCF system has been the most successful in mobilising savings. By the end of 1996 – only two years after coming into operation – the average savings per member amounted to US$170. This is remarkable given that average annual per capita income in rural Vietnam at that time was approximately US$100. Part of the explanation is that the founders and the majority of the rank-and-file members belong to the upper income quintiles. Other factors also undoubtedly contributed to the relatively successful mobilisation of savings: (i) insurance was available for deposits with terms exceeding three months; (ii) the deposit rate offered was higher than that of other financial institutions; (iii) the proximity and relative autonomy of the PCF in combination with the partial local ownership and involvement in management probably lessened the otherwise widespread distrust towards formal financial institutions; and (iv) accessibility and local presence made it convenient to deposit and/or withdraw funds. In addition, paperwork and bureaucracy were kept to a minimum.

Turning to the VBARD and the VBP, the track record is less positive. Generally, both the VBARD and the VBP do not envisage savings and savings accounts as an essential element of their business plan and mode of operation. Consequently, savings are not a prerequisite for obtaining loans, and savings are not automatically included in the assessment of a potential borrower in the two institutions.

CONCLUDING REMARKS

In conclusion, it was found that the government has in effect laid down an explicit division of labour between the different institutions providing financial services to the rural population. In addition, the local communes, people's committees and mass organisations play a crucial role in the identification, screening and follow-up of clients for each type of institution. As a result the initiative to form joint-liability groups and/or contact with potential lenders has come from the institutions themselves. This reflects a top-down approach, most probably originating from a desire to divide the market among the institutions in order to extend their outreach.

The competition and segmentation of the rural financial markets is further hampered by the widespread practice of offering subsidised interest rates. While this approach has been chosen to improve development opportunities for the rural population, the net effects of this policy are likely to be negative and detrimental to the overall purpose of improving the livelihood of rural populations. In addition to restricting the mobilisation of savings, the practice of subsidising interest rates damages customer perception of credit, lowers the overall quality of financial services and reduces the quality of investment projects financed through the financial sector. All this runs counter to the government desire to develop and create growth opportunities for the agricultural sector.

Addressing these problems will involve profound structural changes in the rural financial sector. Long-term political commitment and allocation of resources is imperative. Failure to address either of these problems is, however, likely to have an adverse effect on the efforts of the agricultural sector to remain competitive both nationally and internationally.

NOTES

1 The decollectivisation process was in fact initiated with Decree No. 100 in 1981. It permitted the delegation of production responsibilities to individuals. It was, however, not the intention to replace production cooperatives with family-based production units at this stage.

2 In this context, 'formal institutions' refers to institutions under the jurisdiction of national banking laws, while 'semiformal institutions' covers all formal institutions that are not subject to banking supervision. The PCF system is an example of a semi-formal institution.

3 Three of the seven regions in Vietnam continue to lag behind. These include the Northern Mountains and Midlands, the Central Highlands and the North Central Coast.

4 The VBARD owns and operates two of the financial lease companies mentioned in Chapter 2.

CHAPTER 6

Conclusion

Over the past 20 years the Vietnamese financial sector has undergone irreversible and fundamental changes in the transition from a centrally coordinated to a market-based sector. New markets and new institutions have been established and new legislation is in place. Direct government control of the sector has been abolished and the (still persistent) indirect control has been reduced.

The reform process has been gradual and has from time to time been set on the backburner for a period. This is not unusual. Evidence from other countries undergoing similar transitions testifies that financial liberalisation and deregulation is a lengthy and difficult process. A number of factors suggest that the reform process is likely to be even more prolonged in the case of Vietnam. First, the French civil law tradition may slow down reforms. Second, and perhaps more important, the Vietnamese tradition of consensus governance, in concert with the ruling elite's preference for social and political stability, is also likely to act as a brake on reforms. Third, the extensive links between the state-owned productive sector and the financial sector may also cause reforms in Vietnam to take longer. Finally, the early crises in the process of liberalising the sector (most notably the collapse of the system of credit cooperatives) may also restrict the pace of reforms because it may take a long time to rebuild trust in the formal financial market that in turn could cause newly established markets to take longer to develop.

As a consequence, the recent gradual reactivation of more comprehensive and fundamental reforms may in many respects represent the end of the beginning rather than the beginning of the end of reforms. The majority of the fundamental and far-reaching reforms required is still at an initial stage and/or have yet to be considered. These include the non-performing loans burdening especially the SOCBs and the fact that policy lending (albeit to a lesser degree) appears to continue through the very same banks. Other recurring and still persistent problems are the lack of transparency and the failure to adopt international accounting and auditing standards.

An important decision, which has been touched upon in a number of contexts, is whether Vietnam should opt for the market-based approach (as in the US) or the German-inspired bank-based model. However, as the Vietnamese equities and securities markets are nascent or non-existing the option of a market-based system appears to be a long-term prospect rather than a realistic alternative. In addition, a number of analysts[1] recommend that countries in transition focus on establishing a strong institutional regulatory and supervisory framework instead of perceiving financial sector development as a choice between two competing systems. The underlying rationale for such a strategy is that a strong regulatory and supervisory framework eventually would enable their typically bank-based system to grow prior to the gradual, long-term adaptation and development of a more market-based system. Levine (2002) is able to support the recommendation with recent cross-country empirical analyses indicating that 'neither market-based nor bank-based financial systems are particularly effective at promoting growth'. Instead, Levine suggests that developing and transitional countries should aim at strengthening the rights of investors and the efficiency of contract enforcement. He argues that it is 'less useful to distinguish financial systems by whether they are bank-based or market-based than it is to focus on the specific laws and enforcement mechanisms that govern both debt and equity transactions'.

The analysis presented in this study supports the view that ensuring a timely, fair and transparent supervision and regulation of the financial sector is of central importance to financial sector development and stability. Liberalising financial markets is thus not solely a question of limiting and/or restricting government influence. It might in fact involve the opposite as the influence and power of supervisory and regulatory institutions in many cases needs to be strengthened. As a consequence, the Vietnamese government will continue to play a central role for the financial sector, albeit through different channels of influence.

NOTE

1   See Gibson and Tsakalotos (1994) and Levine (2002).

The state-owned commercial banks

The four SOCBs are the leading banks of the banking system and have 230 branches in all cities and provinces in Vietnam. The number of third-level branches nation-wide is more than a thousand. The number of staff working in the SOCBs is approximately 40,000, of whom the graduate and post-graduate workforce accounts for 55 per cent, while 43 per cent has high school graduation as their highest educational attainment. The remaining 2 per cent include the unskilled workforce.

As mentioned earlier, the group of SOCBs dominates the credit market. At year-end 1999 outstanding loan volume of these four SOCBs accounted for 73 per cent of all loans in the economy. This dominance is mirrored in the mobilisation of funds, where the SOCBs accounted for 75 per cent of all resources mobilised through formal institutions.

The Vietnamese Bank for Agriculture and Rural Development (VBARD) is the largest SOCB in terms of legal capital and has a rather wide scope of operations. It serves a wide range of customers and exerts considerable influence not only upon agriculture production but also on non-agriculture activities in rural areas. According to a 2000 report by the VBARD, total capital of the bank was 55,041 billion dong and total debts 48,548 billion dong, of which medium and long-term loans accounted for 42 per cent.[1] The VBARD also has extended international relations and foreign businesses, and it has received finance from international institutions like ADB, the World Bank and the International Fund for Agricultural Development (IFAD). The VBARD has received and implemented 50 foreign agricultural and rural development projects amounting to a total investment capital of over US$1,300 million. In addition, the VBARD has carried out credit programmes with broader socio-economic perspective and objectives as stipulated by the government. These includes policy credit for non-commercial purposes such as: providing loans to build houses on stilts (over water) in flooded areas of the Mekong River delta and providing loans to reduce the adverse impacts of floods and droughts.

According to the annual report of 2000, the Industry and Commerce Bank of Vietnam (Incombank) had total assets of 48,704 billion dong while total deposits were 40,745 billion. Total debts were 26,224 billion dong, of which medium- and long-term loans accounted for 31.6 per cent. Over the year 2000, the Incombank increased the rate of medium- and long-term loans from 20 per cent at the beginning of the year to 25 per cent of total loans at year-end. These loans were predominantly granted to large government programmes and priority sectors such as the postal services, the communication sectors, the processing industry and the production of construction material. In addition, the Incombank delegated investments and performed credit activities for a range of non-commercial purposes such as lending to reduce adverse impacts of floods, the creation of training funds for poor students and loans to purchase food for reserves.

As for the Foreign Trade Bank of Vietnam (Vietcombank), the 2000 annual report shows that total assets by the end of 2000 were 65,633 billion dong, of which funds in foreign currencies accounted for 74.9 per cent. The total volume of deposits at the Vietcombank was 43,748 billion dong, while total credit lending was 14,421 billion dong, of which medium- and long-term loans accounted for 17.61 per cent.[2] A total of 57.8 per cent of total loan volume was in dong. As is evident by its name, the Vietcombank is primarily involved in trade financing.

Finally, the 1999 annual report of the Vietnamese Bank for Investment and Development (VBID) indicates that its total assets amounted to 39,176 billion dong, of which total loans accounted for dong 28,201 billion.[3] Total deposit volume amounted to 18,379 billion dong in 1999. In addition to undertaking the roles of a multi-functional commercial bank, the VBID was responsible for assisting government-directed development investments. In 1999, the government granted the bank a development investment credit worth 8,335 billion dong. This fund was especially allocated to several big economic programmes directed towards industrialisation and modernisation, including programmes to develop the electricity, petroleum, cement, and rubber industries, or programmes directed towards industries processing agricultural outputs such as sugar cane and seafood.

Among the SOCBs it is mainly the Vietcombank and the VBARD that lend to private enterprises for it is these two banks have an extensive branch network at the district and village levels. Moreover, their respective areas of specialisation (dating back to what was stipulated during the monobank era) are in sectors that have seen rapid growth following the initiation of the Doi Moi reforms.

NOTES

1 According to Article 8 of Decision 1627/2001/QD-NHNN, dated 31 December 2001 short-term loans in Vietnam are defined as having a maturity below 12 months. As for the medium-term loans, their maturity ranges from 12 to 60 months, while long-term loans are defined as those having a maturity above 60 months.

2 This was lower than the share of medium- and long-term loans achieved in both 1998 and 1999.

3 Medium- and long-term debts accounted for 61 per cent total credit from the Vietnamese Bank for Investment and Development.

Important events, 1988–2003

1988
- Decree No.53 transforms the one-tier banking system into a two-tiered system by establishing the four large state-owned specialised commercial banks.
- The legal ban on holding dollars is lifted.

1989
- The dong is devalued.

1990
- A large number of credit cooperatives go bankrupt causing the virtual collapse of the credit cooperative system. By the end of 1990 only 160 of the original 7,000 credit cooperatives are operational.
- Law for the Vietnamese Central Bank confirms the shift to a two-tiered banking system. The SBV is officially made responsible for state management of the banking system and given the duties of a central bank.
- The establishment of private commercial banks and to a lesser degree branch offices and representative offices of foreign banks is permitted.
- The rules governing new entries into the banking system are liberalised.
- The rules on the stipulated sector specialisation of the four major SOCBs are removed.

1991
- The practice of increasing money supply to finance budget deficits is officially abolished.
- Domestic banks are allowed to offer time deposits denominated in foreign currency.

1992
- Tight fiscal and monetary measures cause the rate of inflation to decrease and real interest rates to turn positive.

1993
- Decision 390 permits the pilot establishment of a three-tiered system of local, regional and national People's Credit Funds.

- The domestic inter-bank market is established.
- All forms of subsidised credit to SOEs are officially terminated.
- The insurance market is opened for foreign insurance companies in joint-venture agreements with domestic firms.

1994
- The inter-bank market for foreign currency is established.
- The Bankruptcy Law governing all enterprises is passed and economic courts to hear such cases are established.
- Vietnam joins ASEAN.

1995
- Civil code passed by the National Assembly requires the SBV to clarify rules governing borrowing and lending to commercial banks.
- The insurance market is opened for private 100 per cent domestically owned companies.
- Decree 64 stipulates the statute on organisation and operation of financial companies.

1996
- The property market in Hanoi and Ho Chi Minh City collapses.
- The SBV issues a loan classification system stipulating the grouping of loans into four categories.
- Banks are allowed to set interest rates on dong deposits.

1997
- A 6 per cent devaluation to the US$ (February).
- The East Asian Financial Crisis results in macroeconomic turmoil and crisis throughout the region, leading to considerable currency devaluation and reductions in the growth rates of neighbouring countries.
- A 10 per cent devaluation to the US$ (August).

1998
- The Law on the State Bank comes into effect. The law represents an important step towards separating the SBV from the political system and establishing it as an autonomous entity on a par with the executive, legislative and judiciary branches of government.
- The National Congress ceases to officially influence interest rate levels.
- Commercial banks are required to make provision for loan losses.
- State Bank recapitalisation improves the capital adequacy of the SOCBs.
- More than two-thirds of JSBs fail to meet the minimal requirement on chartered capital. As a consequence, a

number of JSBs come under special control/supervision. Some have their licences revoked, while others are forced to merge with other JSBs.

- The SBV decides upon a 10 per cent devaluation of the official exchange rate to the US$.

1999
- Independent diagnostic audits of the SBV, the SOCBs and the JSBs are completed.
- On the basis of these audits, the government decides to restructure the JSBs first. JSBs are classified into four types and restructuring strategies for each type are developed.
- The Bank Restructuring Committee is established.
- Postal savings system is established. The main function is the provision of savings products to groups that are excluded from accessing the formal financial market. The savings mobilised are subsequently used to finance development projects.
- The income tax rate for the banking system is lowered from 45 to 32 per cent.
- The bank reserve requirement ratio is lowered from 8 to 5 per cent.
- Foreign owned insurance companies are allowed to obtain a licence and enter the Vietnamese market albeit only in selected areas such as life insurance.
- The interest rates on deposits in foreign currency are liberalised.
- The SBV announce that the official rate is abolished, opting instead for a crawling-peg to the US$.

2000
- The national stock exchange opens in Ho Chi Minh City.
- The financial assessments of 48 JSBs are completed. As a result, 13 JSBs are placed under special supervision/control by the SBV, two have their banking licences revoked and one is forced to merge.
- Exchange rate policy and regime is eased.
- Land-use rights and other fixed assets are permitted to be used as loan collateral.
- Using the inter-bank market the SBV initiates more market-based control of end-customer interest rates in the banking sector.

- Interest rate controls on foreign currency deposits are liberalised.
- Foreign balancing requirement for foreign-invested enterprises is lifted.
- The Deposit Insurance Agency (DIA) is established as a separate legal entity. The insurance provided by the DIA is provided to all residents in Vietnam and covers up a maximum of 30 million dong. Deposits in foreign currency are, however, excluded from insurance.
- Decision 488 of November 2000 starts the process of gradually changing Vietnamese accounting standards by requiring that risk provisioning should based on overdue debt and that commercial bank assets should be classified into four groups depending on their assessed risk.

2001
- The Ninth Party Congress signals new commitment towards comprehensive reforms.
- Medium-term SOE reform plan adopted (March). Banking and SOE reform is given priority. Annual targets for SOE equitisations are specified for the first three years.
- IMF initiates the recapitalisation of the four large SOCBs.
- The government announces that policy-induced lending will be phased out 'except under limited and explicitly identified circumstances with government guarantees'.
- Decision 284 officially brings loan classification and loan-loss provisioning in line with international standards.
- Decision 1627 stipulates that the entire loan balance should be classified as overdue if interest and/or principal payments are overdue.
- The interest rate ceilings on foreign currency loans are abolished.
- US–Vietnam bilateral trade agreement is implemented

2002
- A decentralised system of asset management companies is established to face the problem of non-performing loans in the SOCBs.
- Phased recapitalisation of the SOCBs is initiated using comprehensive reviews based on international accounting standards. The process is, however, off to a slow start.

- Banks are allowed to set interest rates for loans through individual assessment of and negotiations with individual customers.
- First tranche of SOCB recapitalisation is released despite all four SOCBs failing to meet the required targets.
- The Registry Centre for Secured Transactions is established.
- A Credit Information Centre assigned with the task of providing information about borrowers to banks is established.
- Lending rates in domestic currency are liberalised.
- Negotiations about Vietnamese membership of the WTO begin.

2003
- The policy lending bank, named the Bank for Social Policies (BSP), is established.
- Second tranche of SOCB recapitalisation is released – again none of the SOCBs meet the required targets.

Bank supervision and regulation indicators

The purpose of this appendix is to present the methodology used by Barth *et al.* (2001) to construct the indicators used in the regional comparison presented in Chapter 2.

Competition regulatory variables (Tables 3.3 and 3.4)

Barth *et al.* (2001) present three variables that qualitatively capture the extent to which competition within the banking industry is restricted. The variables all relate to the ability of existing or new banks to enter the banking business. More specifically, the three variables are defined and quantified as follows.

Limitations on foreign ownership of domestic banks: whether there are any limitations placed on the ownership of domestic banks by foreign banks. If there are any restrictions, this variable is assigned a value of 1 and a value of 0 otherwise.

Limitations on foreign bank entry: whether there are any limitations placed on the ability of foreign banks to enter the domestic banking industry. If there are any restrictions, this variable is assigned a value of 1 and a value of 0 otherwise.

Entry into banking requirements: whether there are specific legal submissions required to obtain a licence to operate as a bank. Barth *et al.* (2001) considered different types of submissions that could be considered by the banking authorities when deciding whether or not to grant a licence. These are as follows:

1. Draft by-laws.

2. Intended organisational chart.

3. First three-year financial projections.

4. Financial information on main potential shareholders.

5. Background/experience of future directors.

6. Background/experience of future managers.

7. Sources of funds to be used to capitalise the new bank.

8. Intended differentiation of new bank from other banks.

Each of these submissions was assigned a value of 1 if it was required and a value of 0 otherwise. This means that the more information required by the regulatory authorities of the type indicated when deciding upon whether or not to issue a licence, the more restrictive will be the entry into banking. The Entry into Banking Requirements variable is created by adding these eight variables together. It therefore may range in value from 0 to 8, with higher values indicating more restrictiveness.

Official supervisory action variable (Tables 3.5 and 3.6).
The following variables was constructed by Barth *et al.* (2001) to capture quantitatively the degree to which supervisory authorities may intervene to promote a 'safe and sound' banking industry.
Official supervisory power: whether the supervisory authorities have the authority to take specific actions to prevent and correct problems. This variable is based upon yes or no responses to the following 16 questions:

1. Can supervisors meet with any external auditors to discuss their reports without bank approval?

2. Are auditors legally required to report any misconduct by managers or directors to the supervisory authorities?

3. Can the supervisory authorities take legal action against external auditors for negligence?

4. Can the supervisory authorities force a bank to change its internal organisational structure?

5. Can the deposit insurance agency take legal action against bank directors or officers?

6. Are off-balance sheet items disclosed to the supervisory authorities?

7. Does failure to abide by a cease-desist type order lead to the automatic imposition of civil and penal sanctions on the directors and managers of a bank?

8. Can the supervisory authorities order a bank's directors/managers to provide provisions to cover actual or potential losses?

9. Can the supervisory authorities suspend the directors' decision to distribute dividends?

10. Can the supervisory authorities suspend the directors' decision to distribute bonuses?

11. Can the supervisory authorities suspend the directors' decision to distribute management fees?

12. Can the supervisory authorities supersede shareholder rights and declare a bank insolvent?

13. Can the supervisory authorities suspend some or all ownership rights of a problem bank?

14. Regarding bank restructuring and reorganisation, can the supervisory authorities supersede shareholder rights?

15. Regarding bank restructuring and reorganisation, can the supervisory authorities remove and replace management?

16. Regarding bank restructuring and reorganisation, can the supervisory authorities remove and replace directors?

The answers to these 16 questions collectively constitute our measure of Official Supervisory Power. Barth *et al.* (2001) specifically assign a value of 1 to a 'yes' answer and a value of 0 to a 'no' answer. This variable is the sum of these assigned values and therefore may range from 0 to 16, with a higher value indicating more power.

Prompt corrective action index: measures whether a law establishes pre-determined levels of bank solvency deterioration that force automatic enforcement actions such as intervention. If this is indeed the case, Barth *et al.* assign a value of 1, 0 otherwise. This is subsequently multiplied by the score obtained from questions (4), (7), (8), (9), (10) and (11) as described above. The prompt corrective action variable may therefore range from 0 to 6, with a higher value indicating more promptness in responding to problems.

Restructuring power index: seeks to quantify whether the supervisory authorities have the power to restructure and reorganise a troubled bank. This variable is simply the sum of the score obtained from questions (14), (15) and (16) as described above. It may range in value from a low of 0 to a high of 3, with a higher value indicating more power.

Insolvency power index: looks at whether the supervisory authorities have the power to declare a deeply troubled bank insolvent. This variable is simply the sum of questions (12) and (13) as described above. It may range in value from 0 to 2, with a higher value indicating greater power.

Bank activity regulatory variables (Tables 3.7 and 3.8)

There are three regulatory variables that affect important activities in which banks may engage. The three variables involve securities, insurance and real estate activities. Barth *et al.* (2001) specifically measure the degree to which the national regulatory authorities in countries allow banks to engage in the following three fee based rather than more traditional interest spread-based activities:

a. **Securities:** the ability of banks to engage in the business of securities underwriting, brokering, dealing, and all aspects of the mutual fund industry.

b. **Insurance:** the ability of banks to engage in insurance underwriting and selling.

c. **Real Estate:** the ability of banks to engage in real estate investment, development and management.

The World Bank and surveys made by the Office of the Comptroller of Currency (OCC) provided information in response to a series of individual questions regarding each country's regulations concerning these activities. Using this information, Barth *et al.* quantified the degree of regulatory restrictiveness for each aggregate or composite activity on a scale from 1 to 4, with larger numbers representing greater restrictiveness. The definitions of the 1 through 4 designations are as follows:

1. **Unrestricted** – a full range of activities in the given category can be conducted directly in the bank.

2. **Permitted** – a full range of activities can be conducted, but all or some must be conducted in subsidiaries.

3. **Restricted** – less than a full range of activities can be conducted in the bank or subsidiaries.

4. **Prohibited** – the activity cannot be conducted in either the bank or subsidiaries.

The difference between a 1 and 2 indicates only the locations in which the activity may be conducted, not whether the activity is restricted in any way.

Mixing banking/commerce regulatory variables (Tables 3.7 and 3.8)
Barth *et al.* (2001) construct two aggregate variables to measure the degree of regulatory restrictiveness on the mixing of banking and commerce. Once again the regulatory restrictiveness for each variable is quantified on a scale from 1 to 4. The specific variable definitions and the definitions of the 1–4 designations are as follows:
Nonfinancial firms owning banks: the ability of non-financial firms to own and control banks.

1. **Unrestricted** – a non-financial firm may own 100 per cent of the equity in a bank.

2. **Permitted** – unrestricted with prior authorisation or approval.

3. **Restricted** – limits are placed on ownership, such as a maximum per cent of a bank's capital or shares.

4. **Prohibited** – no equity investment in a bank.

Banks owning non-financial firms: the ability of banks to own and control nonfinancial firms.

1. **Unrestricted** – a bank may own 100 per cent of the equity in any non-financial firm.

2. **Permitted** – a bank may own 100 per cent of the equity in a non-financial firm, but ownership is limited based on a bank's equity capital.

3. **Restricted** – a bank can only acquire less than 100 per cent of the equity in a non-financial firm.

4. **Prohibited** – a bank may not acquire any equity investment in a non-financial firm.

Capital regulatory variables (Tables 3.9 and 3.10)

Barth *et al.* (2001) list four different capital regulatory variables that capture different but complementary measures of the stringency of regulatory capital requirements across countries. The specific measures are as follows:

Overall capital stringency: the objective is to measure whether there are explicit regulatory requirements regarding the amount of capital that a bank must have relative to various guidelines. Barth *et al.* (2001) consider several guidelines to determine the degree to which the leverage potential for capital is limited. These are as follows:

1. Does the minimum required capital-to-asset ratio conform to the Basle guidelines?

2. Does the minimum ratio vary with market risk?

3. Is the market value of loan losses deducted from reported accounting capital?

4. Are unrealised losses in the securities portfolio deducted from reported accounting capital?

5. Are unrealised foreign exchange losses deducted from reported accounting capital?

Barth *et al.* (2001) assign a value of 1 to each of the above questions if the answer is 'yes' and a 0 otherwise. In addition, a value of 1 is assigned if the fraction of revaluation gains that is allowed to count as regulatory capital is less than 0.75. Otherwise, a value of 0 is assigned. Adding together these variables creates the variable overall capital stringency. It ranges in value from 0 to 6, with higher values indicating greater stringency. Notice that this particular measure of capital stringency is to some degree capturing whether or not regulatory capital is solely an accounting concept or at least partially a market-value concept.

Initial capital stringency: is created to measure whether the source of funds counted as regulatory capital can include assets other than cash or government securities and borrowed funds as well as whether the sources are verified by the regulatory or supervisory authorities. More specifically, the following three questions were asked:

1. Can initial and subsequent infusions of regulatory capital include assets other than cash or government securities?

2. Can the initial infusion of capital be based on borrowed funds?

3. Are the sources of funds that count as regulatory capital verified by the regulatory or supervisory authorities?

A 'yes' is assigned a value of 1. Otherwise, values of 0 are assigned. Adding these three variables together constitutes the measure of initial capital stringency – a variable that may range from a low of 0 to a high of 3, with a higher value indicating less stringency.

References

Acemoglu, D., S. Johnson and J.A. Robinson (2001) 'The colonial origins of comparative development: An empirical investigation', *American Economic Review*, vol. 91, no. 5, pp. 1369–1401.

Appold, S.J. and D.T. Phong (2001) 'Patron–client relationships in a restructuring economy: An exploration of interorganisational linkages in Vietnam', *Economic Development and Cultural Change*, vol. 50, no. 1, pp. 46–75.

Ardener, S. (1965) 'The comparative study of rotating credit associations', *Journal of the Royal Anthropological Institute of Great Britain and Ireland*, vol. 94, no. 2, pp. 201–209.

Asian Development Bank (ADB) (1999) *Rising to the Challenge in Asia: A Study of Financial Markets, Vol. 12: Vietnam*. Manila: Asian Development Bank.

Barth, J.R., G. Caprio and R. Levine (2001a). 'Bank regulation and supervision: What works best?' Working Paper 2725, Washington, DC: The World Bank.

Barth, J.R., G. Caprio and R. Levine (2001b). 'The regulation and supervision of Banks: around the world, a new database'. Working Paper 2588, Washington, DC: The World Bank.

Beck, T., G. Clarke, A. Groff, P. Keefer and P. Walsh, P. (2000). 'New tools and new tests in comparative political economy: The database of political institutions. Working Paper 2283, Washington, DC: The World Bank.

Beck, T., A. Demirgüc-Kunt and R. Levine (2001). 'Law, politics and finance'. Working Paper 2585. Washington, DC: The World Bank.

Beck, T., A. Demirgüc-Kunt, R. Levine and V. Maksimov (2000). 'Financial structure and economic development: Firm, industry, and country evidence'. Working Paper 2423, Washington, DC: The World Bank.

Beckerman, P. (1997) 'Central bank decapitalization in developing countries', *World Development*, vol. 25, no. 2, pp. 167–178.

Besley, T., S. Coate and G. Loury (1993) 'The economics of rotating savings and credit associations', American Economic Review, vol. 83, no. 4, pp. 792–810.

Bongini, P., S. Claessens and G. Ferri (2000) 'The political economy of distress in East Asian financial institutions'. Policy Research Working Paper 2430, Washington DC: The World Bank.

Brownbridge, M. and C. Kirkpatrick, C. (1999) 'Financial sector regulation: The lessons of the Asian crisis'. Institute for Development Policy and Management Working Paper 2, Manchester: University of Manchester.

Camdessus, M. (1999) 'Second generation reforms: Reflections and new challenges'. Opening remarks to IMF conference on second-generation reforms, IMF Headquarters, Washington DC, 8 November.

Claessens, S., A. Demirgüc-Kunt, and H. Huizinga (2001). 'How does foreign entry affect the domestic banking market?', *Journal of Banking and Finance*, vol. 25, no. 5, pp. 891–911.

Cohen, M. (2001a) 'Hard sell', *Far Eastern Economic Review*, 5 April.

Cohen, M. (2001b) 'Second rime around', *Far Eastern Economic Review*, 31 May.

Cohen, M. (2001c) 'Underground', *Far Eastern Economic Review*, 2 August.

Cohen, M. (2003) 'Twinning to reform', *Far Eastern Economic Review*, 25 November.

Cooke, D. and J. Foley (2000) 'The role of the asset management entity: an East Asian perspective'. In *Rising to the Challenge in Asia: A Study of Financial Markets: Volume 2 – Special Issues*, Asian Development Bank, Manila, The Philippines.

Cukierman, A. (1992) *Central bank strategy, credibility and independence: Theory and evidence*. Cambridge, MA: MIT Press.

Dat, T.T. (1998) 'Borrower transaction costs and segmented markets: A study of the rural credit market in Vietnam'. In L. Suiwah (ed.) *Vietnam and the East Asian Crisis*, New York: Edward Elgar Press.

Debelle, G. and S. Fischer (1994) 'How independent should a central bank be?' CEPR Technical Paper, CEPR Publication No. 392, Stanford University, CA.

Demirgüc-Kunt, A. and E. Detragiache (1998) 'Financial liberalisation and financial fragility'. In *Proceedings of the Annual World Bank Conference on Development Economics*, Washington DC: The World Bank.

Demirgüc-Kunt, A. and H. Huizinga (2000) 'Financial structure and bank profitability'. Policy Research Working Paper 2265, Washington D. C.: The World Bank

Diamond, D.,W. (1991) 'Debt, maturity and liquidity risk', *Quarterly Journal of Economics*, vol. 106, no. 3, pp. 709–37.

van Donge, J., H. White and L.X. Nghia (1999) *Fostering Growth in a Low Income Country: Programme Aid to Vietnam*. Stockholm: Sida.

Dung, K.T. (2001) 'Informal credit and its role in the agricultural household economy', (translated from Vietnamese), Mimeo, Hanoi: Central Institute of Economic Management.

Eijffinger, S.C.W. and J. de Haan (1996) 'The political economy of central bank independence'. Princeton Special Papers in International Economics, no. 19, Princeton University Press.

Embassy of the United Kingdom, Hanoi (2001) *Vietnam 2001 Economic Report*. EU Economic and Commercial Counsellors, Hanoi.

Fallavier, P. (1998) 'Developing micro-finance institutions in Vietnam: Policy implications to set up an enabling environment'. MA thesis, University of British Columbia, Canada.

Fforde, A. and S. de Vylder (1996) *From Plan to Market: The Economic Transition in Vietnam*. Boulder: Westview Press.

Foreign Trade Bank of Vietnam (2001) *Annual Report for 2000*, Hanoi, Vietnam.

Freeman, N. (1998) 'Market reality', *Vietnamese Business Journal*, vol. 6, no. 5, pp. 31–3.

Gallup, J.L., J.D. Sachs and A.D. Millinger (1998) 'Geography and economic development'. *Working Paper* 6849, Cambridge, MA: National Bureau of Economic Research.

Geertz, C. (1962) 'The rotating credit association: A middle rung in development', *Economic Development and Cultural Change*, vol. 10, no. 3, pp. 241–63.

Gibson, H. and E. Tsakalotos (1994) 'Limits of financial liberalisation in developing countries: A critical overview', *Journal of Development Studies*, vol. 30, no. 3. pp. 578–628.

Goodman, J.B. (1991) 'The politics of central bank independence', *Comparative Politics*, vol. 23, April, pp. 329–49.

Grilli, V., D. Masciandaro, and G. Tabellini, G. (1991) 'Political and monetary institutions: when are independent central banks irrelevant?' *Economic Policy*, vol. 13, pp. 341–392.

de Haan, J. and W.J. Kooi (2000) 'Does central bank independence really matter? New evidence for developing countries using a new Indicator', Journal of Banking and Finance, vol. 24, no. 4., pp. 643–64.

Hao, T.K *et al.* (1996) 'Assessment of the role of the different types of informal credit vis-à-vis SME Development in Vietnam' (translated from Vietnamese). In Summaries of Recent Research Results under the Vietnamese National Research Programme vol. 1, Hanoi: The Agricultural Publishing Co.

Hellmann, T., K. Murdock, and J. Stiglitz (2000) 'Liberalization, moral hazard in banking and prudential regulation: are capital controls enough?' *American Economic Review*, vol. 90, no. 1, pp. 147–165.

Hermes, N. and R. Lensink (2000) 'Financial system development in transition economies', *Journal of Banking and Finance*, vol. 24, no. 4, pp. 507–524.

Herring, R. J. and N. Chatusripitak (2000) 'The case of the missing market: The bond market and why it matters for financial development'. Institute Working Paper Series, no. 11, Manila: Asian Development Bank.

IMF (1999) *Vietnam – Selected Issues*. Country Report no.99/55, Washington DC: International Monetary Fund.

IMF (2001) *Vietnam: Request for a Three-Year Arrangement under the Poverty Reduction and Growth Facility*. Country Report no. 01/59, Washington DC: International Monetary Fund.

IMF (2003) *Vietnam: Selected Issues*, Washington DC: International Monetary Fund.

IMF and IDA (2001) *Joint Staff Assessment of Interim Poverty Reduction Strategy Paper by the Government of Viet Nam*, Washington DC: The International Monetary Fund and The International Development Association.

Industry and Commerce Bank of Vietnam (2001) *Annual Report for 2000*, Hanoi, Vietnam.

Johnston, B. (1994) 'The speed of financial sector reform: Risks and strategies'. Papers on Policy Analysis and Assessment, no. 9426, Washington DC: IMF and Brookings Institute.

King, R.G. and R. Levine (1993) 'Finance and growth: Schumpeter might be right', *Quarterly Journal of Economics*, vol. 108, no. 3, pp. 717–37.

Klump, R. and K. Gottwald, K. (2003) 'Financial reforms in Vietnam'. In M. Hall (ed.) *The International Handbook on Financial Reform*, Northhampton: Edward Elgar.

Kovsted, J and P. Lyk-Jensen (2000) 'The rotating credit and savings association: The choice between a random or a bidding allocation of funds', *Journal of Development Economics*, vol. 60, no. 1, pp. 143–72.

Kydland, F.W. and E.E. Prescott (1977) 'Rules rather than discretion: The inconsistency of the optimal plans', *Journal of Political Economy*, vol. 85, no. 3, pp. 473–91.

KFW (2002) 'Financial co-operation with Vietnam – financial sector report'. Interim report, Berlin: Kreditanstalt für Wiederaufbau.

La Porta, R., F. Lopez-de-Silanes and A. Shleifer (2002) 'Government ownership of banks', *Journal of Finance*, vol. 57, no. 1, pp. 265–301.

La Porta, R., F. Lopez-de-Silanes, A. Shleifer and R.W. Vishny (1998) 'Law and finance', *Journal of Political Economy*, vol. 106, no. 6, pp. 1113–55.

La Porta, R., F. Lopez-de-Silanes, A. Shleifer and R. W. Vishny (1999) 'The quality of government'. *Journal of Law, Economics and Organisation*, vol. 15, no. 1, pp. 222–279.

Lan, D., P. (2000) 'The Asian financial crisis and its implications for Vietnam's financial system'. Visiting Researchers Series 11, Singapore: Institute of Southeast Asian Studies.

Le Roy, P. and M. Robert (1999) 'The micro-economic impact of rural credit in northern Vietnam – insights from a local situation'. Collection Etudes et Traveaux, Paris: Groupe de recherché e d'échanges technologiques.

Leung, S. and N. Huy Duc (1999) 'Dollarization and financial sector developments in Vietnam'. In S. Leung (ed.) *Vietnam and the East Asian Crisis*, Northhampton, MA: Edward Elgar.

Levine, R. (2002) 'Bank-based or market-based financial systems: Which is better?'. Working Paper, no. 9138, Cambridge, MA: National Bureau of Economic Research.

Llanto, G. (2000) 'Vietnam'. In *The Role of Central Banks in Microfinance in Asia and the Pacific*, Manila: Asian Development Bank.

Lopez, J. A. (1999) 'Using CAMELS ratings to monitor bank conditions', *FRBSF Economic Letter*, vol. 99, no. 19, San Francisco: Federal Reserve Bank of San Francisco.

Mas, I (1995) 'Central bank independence: A critical view from a developing country perspective', *World Development*, vol. 23, no. 10, pp. 1639–52.

McCarthy, A. (2001) 'Governance institutions and incentive structures in Vietnam'. Economics Working Paper Archive at WUSTL, available at http://econwpa.wustl.edu:80/eps/pe/papers/0110/0110002.pdf.

McMillan, J. and C. Woodruf (1999) 'Interfirm relationships and informal credit in Vietnam', *Quarterly Journal of Economics*, vol. 114, no. 4, pp. 1285–320.

Murray, A. (1999) 'Regulation and reform for Vietnamese banks', *Standard & Poor's Credit Week*, 10 February.

Narayan, F. B. and T. Gooden, T. (2000) *Financial Management and Governance Issues in Vietnam*. Manila: Asian Development Bank.

Ninh, L.K. (2003) 'Investment of Rice Mills in Vietnam'. PhD Dissertation, University of Gronningen.

North, D. (1990). *Institutions, Institutional Change, and Economic Performance*. Cambridge: Cambridge University Press.

Oh, S. (1999) 'Financial deepening in the banking sector – Viet Nam'. In *Rising to the Challenge in Asia: A Study of Financial Markets: Volume 12: Socialist Republic of Viet Nam*, Manila: Asian Development Bank.

Olson, M. (1993) 'Dictatorship, democracy, and development'. *American Political Science Review*, vol. 87, no. 3, pp. 567–576.

Park, Y.C. and J.W. Lee (2002) 'Financial crisis and recovery: Patterns of adjustment in East Asia, 1996–99'. Institute Research Paper Series, no. 45, Manila: Asian Development Bank.

Phoung, N. N. (2001) 'Reform can't be bought in Vietnam', *Asia Times* 21 December.

Posen, A.S. (1994) 'Why central bank Independence does not cause low inflation – there is no institutional fix for politics', In R. O'Brien (ed.) *Finance and the International Economy: 7. The Amex Bank Review Prize Essays 1993*. Oxford: Oxford University Press for The Amex Bank Review.

Posen, A.S. (1995) 'Declarations are not enough: Financial sector sources of central bank independence'. In *Macroeconomics Annual,* Cambridge, MA: National Bureau of Economic Research.

Rana, P.B. and N. Hamid (1995) *From Centrally Planned to Market Economies: The Asian Approach, Lao PDR, Myanmar, and Viet Nam, Vol. 3*. Oxford: Oxford University Press.

Rand, J., F. Tarp, Nguyen Huu Dzung and Dao Quang Vinh (2004*) Documentation of the Small and Medium Scale Enterprise (SME) Survey in Vietnam for the Year 2002*, available from authors (e-mail: John.Rand@econ.ku.dk) on request.

Robinson, J. (1980) *The Generalisation of the General Theory*. London: Palgrave-Macmillan.

Rogoff, K. (1985) 'The optimal degree of commitment to an intermediate monetary target', *Quarterly Journal of Economics,* vol. 100, no. 4, pp. 1169–89 .

Shimomoto, Y. (1999) 'Developing the capital market – Viet Nam'. In *Rising to the Challenge in Asia: A Study of Financial Markets: Volume 12: Socialist Republic of Viet Nam*, Manila: Asian Development Bank.

Siregar, R. (1999) 'Management of macroeconomic policies – Viet Nam'. In *Rising to the Challenge in Asia: A Study of Financial Markets: Volume 12: Socialist Republic of Viet Nam*, Manila: Asian Development Bank.

Socialist Republic of Vietnam (2001a) 'Letter of intent, memorandum of economic and financial policies of the government of Vietnam for 2001'. Washington DC: International Monetary Fund.

Socialist Republic of Vietnam (2001b) 'Interim poverty reduction strategy paper'. Hanoi: Ministry of Finance.

Socialist Republic of Vietnam (2002) 'Letter of intent, memorandum of economic and financial policies, and technical memorandum of understanding'. Submitted to the IMF, Hanoi.

State Bank of Vietnam (2000). *Banking Legislation in Vietnam*. Hanoi: State Bank of Vietnam.

Sturm, J.-E. and J. de Haan (2001) 'Inflation in Developing Countries: Does Central Bank Independence Matter?'. Working Paper no. 511, Munich: CESifo.

Thayer, C. (2000) 'Vietnam, the Asian Financial Crisis and Doi Moi 2', *Harvard Asia Quarterly*, available at http://www.fas.harvard.edu/~asiactr/haq/200001/0001a003.htm.

Thong, B., N. (2003) 'Tackling disputes on the Vietnamese insurance market: A case study of the Bao Viet Insurance company '. MA Thesis, Hanoi: National University of Hanoi.

Toan, D. Q., L. T. Tam, N. T. V. Nga and D. L. Tan (2001) 'Credit'. Chapter 13 in *Living Standards during an economic boom: Vietnam 1993–1998*. United Nations Development Program and Statistical Publishing House, Hanoi, Vietnam.

Tou, T.B. (2001) 'The orientation of and visions for banking supervision' (translated from Vietnamese), *Banking Magazine,* vol. 9, pp. 4–7.

Trong, L.H. (2002) 'Recapitalization of Vietnamese SOCBs' *Vietnamese Banking Review*, no. 13., October, pp. 5–9.

Unteroberdoerster, O. (2002) 'Foreign currency deposits in Vietnam: Trends and policy issues'. In *Vietnam: Selected Issues and Statistical Appendix*, IMF Country Report no. 02/5, Washington DC: International Monetary Fund.

Rajan, R. S. and G. Bird (2001) 'Still the weakest link: The domestic financial system and post 1998 recovery in East Asia', *Development Policy Review*, vol. 19, no. 3, pp. 355–66.

Reisen, H. (1998) 'Domestic causes of currency crises: Policy lessons for crisis avoidance'. Technical paper 136, OECD Development Centre, Paris: Organisation for Economic Co-operation and Development.

Vietnam–Sweden Mountain Rural Development Programme (1999) *A Synthesis of Participatory Poverty Assessments from Four Sites in Viet Nam: Lao Cai, Ha Tinh, Tra Vinh & Ho Chi Minh City*, submission to the WDR 2000, Hanoi.

Vietnamese Bank for Agriculture and Rural Development (2001) *Annual Report for 2000*. Hanoi.

Vietnamese Bank for Investment and Development (2000) *Annual Report for 1999*. Hanoi.

Wolff, P. (ed.) (1999) *Vietnam – The Incomplete Transition*, London: Frank Cass Publishers.

Woo-Cumings, M. (2001) 'Diverse paths toward 'the right institutions': Law, the state, and economic reform in East Asia'. Institute Working Paper Series, no. 18, Manila: Asian Development Bank..

World Bank (1995) *Viet Nam Financial Sector Review: An Agenda for Financial Sector Development*. Washington DC: The World Bank.

World Bank (2001) *World Development Report*. Washington DC: The World Bank.

World Bank (2001) *Vietnam Development Report 2002: Implementing Reforms for Faster Growth and Poverty Reduction*. Hanoi: World Bank.

World Bank (2002a) *World Development Report 2002: Building Institutions for Markets*. Washington DC: World Bank.

World Bank (2002b) *Banking Sector Review, Vietnam*. Washington DC: World Bank.

World Bank (2003) *Vietnam: Delivering on Its Promise, Vietnam Development Report 2003*. Hanoi: World Bank.

World Development Indicators (2002) *The World Development Indicators CD-Rom*. Washington DC: World Bank

Index

1997 Financial Crisis. *See* East Asian Financial Crisis

accountability, lack of
  as cause of EAFC 2
  effect of civil law tradition 3
  measures against 45, 63
  as obstacle to financial sector liberalisation xviii, 53

accounting standards 145
  current (Vietnamese) 20, 37–38, 43, 44; deficiencies in ~ 43–45, 116, 136
  international ~ , adoption of 44–45, 116, 136
  see also banks, domestic

agricultural sector
  banks in xxi, 121–128, 131–132. *See also* state-owned commercial banks; Vietnam Bank of Agriculture and Rural Development; Vietnam Bank for the Poor; Vietnamese Bank for Investment and Development
  credit 14–17. *See also* credit; credit cooperatives; People's Credit Funds; Vietnam Bank of Agriculture and Rural Development
  decollectivisation 10, 15, 122, 133n
  development opportunities xxii
  government policies towards xxii, 14, 16, 132–133. *See also* government policies
  increased demand for financial services 122
  loans, crucial role of communes etc. in xxii, 124, 127
  see also liberalisation, financial sector

Asian Development Bank 114, 127, 139

Asian Financial Crisis. *See* East Asian Financial Crisis

asset management companies 106–117, 145
  autonomy 113
  funding 114–115
  powers 113–114
  and SOCBs 111–112
  types 106, 108

assets
  as collateral for loans. *See* collateral
  high liquidity of 131
  management. *See* asset management companies
  see also land; savings

audits. *See* banks, domestic

autonomy. *See* asset management companies; state-owned commercial banks; State Bank of Vietnam

Bank of Agriculture and Rural Development. *See* Vietnam Bank of Agriculture and Rural Development

Bank for Foreign Trade. *See* Vietcombank

Bank for Investment and Development. *See* Vietnamese Bank for Investment and Development

Bank for the Poor. *See* Vietnam Bank for the Poor

Bank for Social Policies   46, 146. *See also* lending, policy-based; non-performing loans

banking sector
  in central planning period   2, 8–10
  competition within. *See* competition, financial sector
  concentration   61, 63, 75. *See also* competition, financial sector
  entry. *See* entry, banking sector
  government restrictions on   xx, 69, 70–72, 124
  increased foreign presence. *See* banks, foreign
  likely impact of indirect regulation   xix, 82
  move to two-tier system   12, 142
  safety nets   72–74
  see also banks, commercial; banks, domestic; banks, foreign; financial sector; informal financial sector; regulatory framework

banks, commercial
  legalised   12
  types   12. *See also* banks, foreign; credit cooperatives; JSB; JVB; state-owned commercial banks

banks, domestic
  activities limited by government   xx, xxi, 124
  in agricultural sector   xxi, 15–16, 121–128, 131–132
  auditing of   44–45
  capital, asset, management, earnings and liquidity (CAMEL)   102, 118
  capital requirements   xx, 74
  fragility   59, 63, 72, 74, 75, 128
  franchise value of   xix, 58, 72, 128

lack of competition between. *See* competition, financial sector
  state ownership of   9
  viability dependent on resolving NPL issue   20
  see also banks, commercial; state-owned banks; state-owned commercial banks

banks, foreign   31n
  concerns about   62
  effect on domestic financial sector   62, 63
  entry permitted   12
  increased presence   xix, xx, 13, 18, 61–62, 89, 116
  restrictions on   18
  US   xix, 51

Bilateral Trade Agreement (between Vietnam and USA)   xix, 40, 51, 62, 75, 89, 145. *See also* banks, foreign; financial markets

bond market   90–95, 117n–118n
  deficiencies in   xx–xxi, 90–91, 93, 116
  importance of   90. *See also* savings
  internationalisation of   93–95. *See also* foreign direct investment
  used to finance government deficits   xxi, 91
  see also treasury bills

capital adequacy ratio   47, 48. *See also* state-owned commercial banks

central bank. *See* State Bank of Vietnam

Central Credit Fund   16–17. *See also* People's Credit Funds

collateral
  laws on   109
  used (or not used) for loans   35, 49, 106, 109, 111, 113, 123, 126, 127, 144. *See also* bond market; loans/lending; non-performing loans; state-owned enterprises
  see also land; savings

communes, crucial role with bank
clients xxi–xxii, 124, 127
Communist Party. *See* Vietnamese
Communist Party
competition, financial sector
effect of foreign banks 62–63
lack of ~ in rural financial
markets xxii, 121, 124, 128, 132
level of xix, 60, 62–63, 65–66, 75
measures of 60–61
see also banking sector; entry,
banking sector; financial sector;
rural financial markets
competition, political. *See* political
competitiveness
consensus governance xiii, 9, 41, 42,
117n
as a brake on reforms xvii, xviii, 53,
54, 135
hinders autonomy of SBV xx, 79, 87,
116
and resolution of NPLs 54
corruption 21, 72
measures against 55n, 98
in other countries 59
credit
in agricultural sector 14–19. *See
also* credit cooperatives; People's
Credit Funds; Vietnam Bank of
Agriculture and Rural Development; Vietnam Bank for the Poor
customer perception of xxii, 129, 132
demand for 15, 48, 122
government control of 17, 18, 20–
21, 124
informal 26–30. *See also* informal
financial sector
SOE share of 18–19, 46, 123
trader 29–30
see also leasing; lending, policy-
based; loans/lending
credit cooperatives 14–16
permitted 12

rapid growth 15
replaced by PCFs 16. *See also*
People's Credit Funds
system collapses xvii–xviii, 15–16,
53, 122, 131, 135, 142
Credit Information Centre 146
crises, financial
EAFC. *See* East Asian Financial Crisis
government role to prevent 57. *See
also* government influence/inter-
vention
greater stability from presence of
foreign banks 61
linked to liberalisation 58
in rural credit. *See* credit
cooperatives
currency
devaluation of dong. *See* dong
foreign. *See* currency, foreign
markets. *See* interbank currency
market
parallel system 23–24
reforms 10, 144, 145
role of SBV 12
currency, foreign
attraction of vs dong 23. *See also*
saving
holdings 23–25, 31n, 32n, 131, 142
interest rates 50, 144, 145. *See also*
interest rate
market 50–51. *See also* interbank
currency market
savings in 49. *See also* savings

debt. *See* credit; loans/lending; non-
performing loans
decollectivisation. *See* agricultural
sector
deposit insurance 49–50, 74–76, 131.
See also Deposit Insurance Agency
Deposit Insurance Agency 49, 145
deregulation. *See* liberalisation, financial
sector; regulatory framework

development, financial system. *See* financial system

Development Assistance Fund   46. *See also* lending, policy-based

Doi Moi. *See* liberalisation, financial sector; reform process

donor community   129

dollars, dollarisation. *See* currency, foreign

dong (VND)
   defending   95
   devaluation   23, 33, 34, 51, 95, 142, 143, 144
   and interest rates   50. *See also* interest rates

East Asian Financial Crisis, 1997–98   21, 33–39, 41, 53, 63, 106, 143
   causes   2, 94, 95
   impact on reform process   xi, 38, 39, 53
   Vietnamese response to   xviii, 35, 53

economic reforms
   driving growth and development   xi
   see also liberalisation, financial sector; reform process

entry, banking sector
   foreign banks permitted   12
   liberalisation of process   xix, 76, 142
   new entrants   xix, 75
   regional comparison   64–65
   restrictions   63–66
   see also banking sector; competition, financial sector; rural financial markets

equitisation
   of banks   xix, 48, 89
   of SOEs   45

Euro. *See* bond market; currency, foreign

financial lease companies   40, 41, 124, 133n. *See also* leasing

financial markets, domestic
   division of labour within   xxi, 124, 132
   management by SBV   xx, 12, 50–51, 89–90, 95–104, 116
   opened to foreign banks   xix, 12, 62–63
   rural. *See* rural financial markets
   state organisation of. *See* government influence/intervention
   see also bond market; interbank currency market; stock exchange/market

financial sector
   analysis, framework for   xiii–xiv
   in central planning period   2, 8–10
   central role of government in   xxii, 57
   at centre of current reform process   xi
   colonial legacy   2–4, 6–8
   competitive pressure within. *See* competition, financial sector
   deregulation. *See* liberalisation, financial sector; regulatory framework
   development influenced by geography   5–7; ~ political factors   4–5; legal system   2–4. *See also* legal system
   direct government control previously   xi, xvii, 8, 135
   diversification   41, 55n
   indirect government control persists xi–xii, 135. *See also* government influence/intervention
   informal. *See* informal financial sector
   investment projects, reduced quality xxii, 132
   lack of transparency. *See* transparency
   'level playing field'   xix, xxii, 62, 75. *See also* competition, financial sector; regulatory framework
   links with state-owned productive sector. *See* state-owned commercial banks: links with SOEs

market-based vs bank-based   136
need for separate regulatory
authority   xxi. *See also* State
Bank of Vietnam
reforms. *See* liberalisation, financial
sector; reform process
regulation. *See* government influence/
intervention; regulatory framework
stability   59, 63. *See also* crises,
financial
trust in   xviii, 16, 22, 49, 53, 90, 131,
135. *See also* Deposit Insurance
Agency
see also banking sector
Financial Sector Restructuring
Authority   108
financial services   39, 46, 60, 62, 89
in agricultural sector   37, 121–133
demand for   37
lowered quality   xxii, 128, 130, 132
supply of   16, 30, 55n
foreign companies   40, 51. *See also*
banks, foreign; insurance market
foreign direct investment (FDI)   33,
34, 94, 95. *See also* bond market;
equitisation
French legal heritage
as brake on reform process   xvii, 53
effect on economic growth   2–4, 8
nature of   2–4
see also financial sector: colonial
heritage; ~ : development

gold   23, 90, 131. *See also* savings
government   55n
bonds. *See* bond market
budget deficits   xxi, 91
concern to preserve social and
political stability. *See* stability
secrecy   34. *See also* transparency
use of financial sector for own
ends   xi

see also consensus governance;
government influence/interven-
tion; government policies; lending,
policy-based; state, role of
government influence/intervention
control of credit allocation. *See* credit
direct vs indirect influence   xx, xxii,
82–83, 116, 124, 136
limiting   xxii, 136
pressure on banks   47, 59, 66, 122,
129. See also lending, policy-based
previous direct control of financial
sector   xi, xvii, 8, 135
restrictions on banking sector   xx, 124
role in financial sector   xxii, 57, 58,
124, 137
see also regulatory framework
government policies
agricultural sector   xxii, 14
to create effective financial environment   57
'uncollected bill' for past failures   xiii,
59, 104

Hui. See Rosca
hyperinflation   10. *See also* inflation

Incombank   140
established   12
recapitalization   47
Industry and Commerce Bank of
Vietnam. *See* Incombank
inflation   10, 11, 80–82, 89
informal financial sector   1, 25–30.
See also credit; loans/lending;
moneylenders; Roscas
insurance market
banks excluded from   xx, 55n, 70,
71, 76
entry of foreign companies   40, 55n,
144
opened   39–40, 55n, 143

inter-bank currency market
  deficiencies in   xx–xxi, 96, 116
  domestic   95–96, 143
  foreign   33, 96, 143
intercorporate debt. *See* non-performing
  loans; state-owned enterprises
interest rates   11, 30, 93, 94, 95, 142
  deregulation of   50, 59, 143, 146
  subsidised   9, 121, 129, 131;
    negative impact of ~   xxii, 129–
    131, 132; positive impact of ~   130
international accounting standards.
  See accounting standards
International Fund for Agricultural
  Development   139
International Monetary Fund   35, 41
investment
  foreign. *See* foreign direct investment
  negative impact of subsidised
    interest rates   xxii, 129

joint-liability groups   xxii, 127, 132
joint-stock banks   18, 54n, 143–144
  debts   31n, 36
  difficulties   36
  growth   13
  permitted   12
  restructured   36, 144
joint-venture banks
  basis   17
  growth   13
  permitted   12

lack of skills. *See* skills
lack of transparency. *See* transparency
land
  as collateral for loans   29, 109
  decollectivisation. *See* agricultural
    sector
  as form of savings/investment   131.
    See also savings
  laws   121
  ownership   109

land-use rights   29, 51, 109, 126, 144
leasing   40–41, 133n
  as form of credit   41
legal system
  deficiencies re land ownership   109
  and financial sector development   2–4
  French heritage. *See* French legal
    heritage
  reform   4, 72
  requirements   57, 63
  see also regulatory framework; State
    Bank of Vietnam
LEIPC. *See* political competitiveness
lending, policy-based   39, 145
  government pressure for   47, 124.
    See also government influence/
    intervention
  as obstacle to financial sector
    liberalisation   xviii, 136
  as hindrance to equitisation   xix
  persistence of   xxi, 46–47, 53, 66
  see also Bank for Social Policies;
    Development Assistance Fund;
    loans/lending; non-performing
    loans
liberalisation, financial sector   53
  achievements   59–60
  crises   xvii, 57. *See also* credit
    cooperatives; crises, economic
  increased pace of since 2001   41, 135
  lengthy process   14, 52, 59
  negative impact   58–59, 128
  obstacles   xviii, 14, 135
  perceived benefits   58, 128
  preceding SOE sector reforms   14
  progress from regional
    perspective   xviii–xix, 53
  see also interest rates; reform process
loans/lending   141n
  crucial role of communes etc.   xxii,
    124, 127
  dominance of SOCBs   139. *See also*
    state-owned commercial banks

by family/friends 28, 30
international. *See* bond market
non-performing. *See* non-performing
loans
rolling over of SOE debt 20, 44
see also collateral; credit; lending,
policy-based; Local Credit Funds;
moneylenders; People's Credit
Funds; Roscas; Vietnam Bank of
Agriculture and Rural Development; Vietnam Bank for the Poor
Local Credit Funds 16–17, 36, 37,
128. *See also* People's Credit Funds

mass organisations 122
crucial role with bank clients xxi–
xxii, 124, 126, 127, 130, 132
Ministry of Finance 46, 112
Ministry of Planning and Investment 112
moneylenders 26, 29, 30

non-performing loans 48, 53, 136
concerns about xii, 20, 104–105
as hindrance to equitisation xix; ~
to SOE reform 104
initial response to problem 105
measures addressing xxi, 44–45, 49,
108, 111–112. *See also* asset
management companies; State
Bank of Vietnam
no speedy resolution xviii, 53
regional comparison 106, 107
understated 20. *See also* transparency
see also lending, policy-based; state-
owned commercial banks; state-
owned enterprises
NPLs. *See* non-performing loans

PCFs. *See* People's Credit Funds
people's committees
crucial role with bank clients xxi–
xxii, 124, 127

People's Credit Funds 36–37, 125–126,
128, 133n
customers 125, 128
established 16, 122, 125, 142. *See
also* credit cooperatives
financial products 126
success of 131–132
see also Central Credit Fund; credit;
loans/lending; Local Credit Funds;
Regional Credit Funds
political competitiveness 5, 6
Prime Minister's Office 112
private enterprises
credit to 15, 18–19, 104, 141
see also equitisation
private lobby group 89
privatisation
of agricultural sector. *See* agricultural
sector
of banks. *See* equitisation
prompt corrective power index 67–69.
See also regulatory framework;
State Bank of Vietnam

Radhanasin Bank 108
real estate 90, 150
banks excluded from ~ market xx,
70, 71, 76, 150
as collateral for loans 106, 126
as form of savings/investment 131.
See also savings
see also agricultural sector; land
reform process
hindered by concerns to preserve
stability. *See* stability
hindered by French civil law heritage
xvii, 53, 135
financial sector now at centre of xi
gradual pace of xvii, 52
initiated 10–13
slowdown after Financial Crisis xi, 52
see also liberalisation, financial sector

Regional Credit Funds   16, 36. *See also*
  People's Credit Funds
Registry Centre for Secured Transactions
  (RCST)   49, 146
regulatory framework
  authority to act   67–68, 84
  bank supervision and regulatory
    indicators   147–153
  benefits of strengthening   xx
  global pressure to strengthen   54
  new rules/legislation not strictly
    enforced   xviii, 53
  regional comparison   xx, 53 68, 85
  requirements   57, 63, 76, 136
  SBV supervision   xx, 97–104; ~ not up
    to international standards   101–
    102
  speed of response to problems   xx,
    xxii, 67, 69, 84–85
  see also State Bank of Vietnam
Rosca (Rotating Savings and Credit
  Association)   26–28. *See also* credit
Rotating Savings and Credit Association. *See* Rosca
rural financial markets   128
  competition in   xxii, 124, 132. *See
    also* competition, financial sector
  early disaster in. *See* credit coopera-
    tives
  segmentation of   xxii, 132. *See also*
    government influence/intervention
  structural changes   xxii, 133
  see also agricultural sector; financial
    markets, domestic; People's Credit
    Funds; Vietnam Bank of Agri-
    culture and Rural Development;
    Vietnam Bank for the Poor
rural sector. *See* agricultural sector

savings   130–132
  alternatives   90. *See also* currency,
    foreign; gold; land

loss of ~ due to credit cooperatives
  crisis   15; ~ leads to mistrust of
  banks   15, 49, 131. *See also*
  assets; credit cooperatives
mobilisation   xxii, 22–23, 39, 121,
  129–131, 144
security of. *See* deposit insurance
  scheme
see also assets; collateral; currency;
  interest rate; Vietnam Postal
  Service Savings Company
SBV. *See* State Bank of Vietnam
securities market   136, 150
  banks excluded from   xx, 70, 71, 72,
    76, 150
seignorage   24, 32n
skills
  building   48, 88, 115
  lack/shortage of   17, 21, 39, 115, 130
small- and medium-scale enterprises
  15. *See also* agricultural sector
SOE. *See* state-owned enterprises
stability, concern for preservation of
  social and political
  as a brake on reforms   xvii
  government priority   xiii, xvii, xviii
state, role of
  as organizer of financial sector   xxii
  see also government; government
    influence/intervention;
    government policies
State Bank of Vietnam
  autonomy/indepedence   xx, 1, 63,
    80–89, 103, 116; ~ types of   82,
    83, 116, 117n
  established   8
  governors   86–87
  influence of government/local
    authorities   84. *See also* govern-
    ment influence/intervention
  management of financial markets   xx,
    12, 50–51, 89–90, 95–104, 116

measures to resolve NPLs   xx, xxi, 104.
  See also non-performing loans
reorganisation   13
role   8, 12, 37–38, 79, 84, 96–97. *See*
  also regulatory framework
separation from banking operations
  12–13, 79, 103. *See also* state-
  owned commercial banks; ~ from
  political system   37, 38, 79, 81,
  82–83. *See also* government
  influence/intervention
staff training   87–88
state-owned banks   12
state-owned commercial banks   13,
  139–141
autonomy   12, 47, 60, 63
banks. *See* Bank for Social Policies;
  Incombank; Vietcombank; Vietnam
  Bank of Agriculture and Rural
  Development; Vietnam Bank for
  the Poor
creation   12
crisis among   35
dominance of   17, 139
lending   48–49; policy-based ~   46,
  47. *See also* lending, policy-based;
  loans/lending
links with SOEs   xvii, 18, 20, 21, 53.
  See also state-owned enterprises
non-performing loans of   35, 43–44,
  104–105, 111–112, 136. *See also*
  non-performing loans
plans to equitise   xix, 48, 49
reform   48, 110, 145; cost of ~   48;
  pressure for ~   42–43; ~ impeded
  by NPLs   104, 136. *See also*
  liberalisation, financial sector;
  reform process
recapitalisation   1, 43, 47–48, 114,
  145, 146
separation from political/state
  authorities. *See* government
  influence/intervention; ~ from
  regulatory authorities. *See* State
  Bank of Vietnam

see also agricultural sector; banking
  sector; banks, domestic; financial
  sector
state-owned enterprises   9
banking sector support during
  Financial Crisis   35
delayed reform of   13–14
equitisation of. *See* equitisation
get most of credit   18
NPL problem among   xviii, 44, 45,
  54, 104, 109
policy based lenging   147–148
pressure for reform   42, 145
slow pace of reform   46
state ownership/control
degree of   60–61
negative effects of   xviii, 61
see also equitisation; government;
  non-performing loans; State Bank
  of Vietnam
State Security Commission   38
stock exchange/market   38–39, 144.
  See also financial markets, domestic

taxes   2, 32n, 35, 44, 109, 144. *See*
  also seignorage
transparency, lack of   128–129
in decision making   9, 42
effect of civil law tradition   3
and financial sector development   xxii
in NPL problem   xviii, 44, 53, 113
needed in opening up of banking
  sector   xix
as obstacle to financial sector
  liberalisation   xviii, 53, 136
as result of financial sector reform
  preceding SOE reform   14
World Bank 'joint reviews', unavail-
  ability of   xii–xiii
treasury bills (T-Bills)   91–93, 116

United States   xix

banks. *See* banks, foreign
bilateral trade agreement with. *See*
    Bilateral Trade Agreement

VBARD. *See* Vietnam Bank of
    Agriculture and Rural Development
Vietcombank   140
    established   9, 12
    importance of   118n–119n
    loans   141
    restructuring of   112
    see also state-owned commercial
        banks
Vietnam Bank of Agriculture and Rural
    Development   46, 121, 125–126,
    132, 133n, 139–140
    customers   123, 125, 127, 141
    established   12, 122, 125
    financial products   126, 133n
    largest bank   122–123, 139
    loans   122–124
    purpose   15, 125
    strengthened   16
    see also agricultural sector; state-
        owned commercial banks
Vietnam Bank for the Poor   46, 125–
    126, 132
    customers mainly the poor   125, 127,
        128
    established   122, 125
    financial products   126
    loans   126, 127, 129, 132

problematic policies   129, 132
purpose   125
see also lending, policy-based; state-
    owned commercial banks
Vietnam Industrial and Commercial
    Bank. *See* Incombank
Vietnamese accounting standards. *See*
    accounting standards
Vietnamese Bank for Investment and
    Development   112, 119n, 140–141
    established   9, 12
    see also state-owned commercial
        banks
Vietnamese Communist Party   9, 42.
    See also government
Vietnamese Living Standards Survey
    (VLSS)   131
Vietnam Postal Service Savings
    Company   39, 46, 144. *See also*
    savings

World Bank   39, 60, 139
    1995 report   xii, 98
    2002 Banking Sector Review   xii, 39,
        46
    'joint reviews', unavailability of. *See*
        transparency, lack of
    pressure for reforms   35, 41
World Trade Organisation
    membership   51, 89, 146